ECONOBABBLE

ECONOBABBLE

How to decode
political spin and
economic nonsense

Richard Denniss

Published by Black Inc.,
an imprint of Schwartz Books Pty Ltd
Level 1, 221 Drummond Street
Carlton VIC 3053, Australia
enquiries@blackincbooks.com
www.blackincbooks.com

9781760643225 (paperback)
9781925203806 (ebook)

 A catalogue record for this
book is available from the
National Library of Australia

Cover and text design by Tristan Main
Typesetting by Typography Studio
Cover illustration www.CartoonStock.com

Printed in Australia by McPherson's Printing Group.

Contents

Introduction

What Is Econobabble?

*'If I turn out to be particularly clear, you've probably
misunderstood what I've said.'*

**—Alan Greenspan, former governor of
the US Federal Reserve**[1]

Economics is like a tyre lever: it can be used to solve a problem, or to beat someone over the head. It's not the tyre lever that is good or bad – it's the person who wields it, and what they try to do with it.

Scott Morrison has made the distinction between 'good' and 'bad' central to his approach to economic management. According to the prime minister: 'Australians understand taking out a mortgage to pay for their home is a wise investment for their future. But they also know that putting your everyday expenses on the credit card is not a good idea. It doesn't end well. This is basically the difference between good and bad debt. The same is true for government.'[2]

Except, of course, it's not. Sometimes it makes sense to put your groceries on your credit card, especially if your car just broke down and needs repairs. And sometimes borrowing to buy a house is a bad idea, especially if you are borrowing to buy a house in a mining town at the end of a mining boom. Making choices is not easy, and while economics is all about the science of decision-making, that doesn't mean economists know what is right and what is wrong – and it certainly doesn't mean we know what the 'best' thing to do is, for a person, a company or a country.

Australia is one of the richest countries in the world. We can afford to do almost anything that any other country can do, but we can't afford to do everything that every other country can do. We have to make choices, hard choices.

Economics has some simple but powerful analytical tools that can be used to help us make those choices, but no economist, and no economic model, can tell us what we 'should' or 'must' do. Like a waiter explaining a menu, economists can help explain the choices available, and can help us understand the cost of the different options, but just as it is not the job of a waiter to tell us what to eat, it is not the job of economists to tell us what we must do.

But economics is not just a set of analytical tools – it is also a powerful language that can conceal simple truths from the public. I call this language 'econobabble', and it includes two things: incomprehensible economic jargon, and apparently simple words that have been stripped of their normal meanings. When public figures and commentators use this sort of language in order to dress up their self-interest as the national interest, to make the absurd seem inevitable or the inequitable seem fair, or even to make the destructive seem prudent, they are econobabbling.

Every day, econobabble is used by powerful people to silence democratic debate about our nation's priorities and values, and to conceal the full range of policy options that we have at our disposal. As the COVID-19 crisis has shown, Australia can afford to provide free childcare and to significantly increase unemployment benefits, and we all now know that there is nothing 'reckless' about running a large budget deficit. But for decades, econobabble has been used to hide these simple truths from the public. The aim of this book is to expose the stupid arguments, bizarre contradictions and complete lack of evidence which econobabble is designed to conceal.

I am sorry to say it, but in our nation today confidence is usually more important than qualifications. Bad economic arguments, without the faintest theoretical or empirical foundation, dominate public debate. Take Scott Morrison, for example. When asked by Leigh Sales, 'Where is your evidence that higher taxes weaken an economy?', the prime minister responded: 'Well, I think it's just fundamental Economics 101, Leigh.'[3]

But, of course, it's not. Such an opinion isn't 'fundamental', and no 'Economics 101' textbook teaches students any such thing. Moreover, the claim is demonstrably wrong. The highest-taxed countries in the world, the Nordic nations, have some of the highest levels of income, life expectancy and happiness.[4]

When nonsense is repeated often enough – especially by prime ministers, well-paid lobbyists, commentators and businesspeople – it can start to seem as though everyone believes that black is white or up is down, especially in the post-truth world of social media. After enough exposure to econobabble, you might even come to think that the best way to help poor people is to give tax cuts to the rich.

This book won't train you as an economist. (Given the lack of qualifications of most people who spout econobabble, however, that shouldn't worry you too much.) But it will give you the evidence, the arguments and, most importantly, the confidence to question assertions you might once have simply accepted, or lacked the confidence to challenge.

This book is for those who, deep down, have never believed that it makes sense, economic or otherwise, to help poor people by slashing public spending on the services they rely on. It's for those who have a sneaking suspicion that it would be cheaper and better to avoid climate change and COVID-19 than to let them rip and cope with the consequences. And it's for those who think it would be more efficient to reduce unemployment than to ship jobs offshore. It will show you how to take on those who pride themselves on being 'great economic managers' but then do nothing more than blame the unemployed for the lack of jobs – and then use dodgy algorithms to try to collect 'robodebts'.

I'm not trying to convince you that economics is stupid – I don't think it is. But I am trying to convince you to join the fight against people who use econobabble to conceal their self-interest. Just as you don't need a black belt in karate to call out bullying when you see it, you don't need an economics degree to call out bullshit when you hear it. Until enough of us name econobabble for what it is, our public debate will never have room for good ideas based on evidence, logic and our collective values.

This second edition comes five years after the first. When I finished writing the first edition in late 2015, it was hard to imagine that Donald Trump would be elected president of the United States, that Scott Morrison would become the prime minister of Australia, or that the COVID-19 pandemic would smash into so many lives and into the global economy. But while those three shocks are largely unrelated, they all come wrapped up in enormous amounts of econobabble, which, unless it is unpacked, will conceal the real choices, and the real motivations, of those we elect to represent us.

Economists don't have all the answers. There is nothing in our theories or our data that can tell you, or a prime minister, what the 'best' tax, health, education or transport system is. Our training does not equip us to know what kind of society you want – it merely helps us to identify the likely costs and the likely benefits of different choices.

The ultimate irony of using econobabble to convince people that 'there is no choice' when it comes to what is 'good for the economy' is that economics is, literally, all about helping people to make such choices. While Economics 101 does not teach students that tax is bad for the economy, it does teach students that they should never tell people what is good for them, and that they should always ask them what they want. Econobabble is the opposite of economics: it conceals choices and impedes genuine democratic debate about priorities. That's why we need to decode it, and that's why I have updated this book.

The Language of Deception

Before taking on the role of 'managing the Australian economy', Scott Morrison worked in tourism marketing. Malcolm Turnbull was a lawyer. Tony Abbott dabbled in journalism and the priesthood, Ben Chifley was an engine driver and John Howard was a suburban solicitor. Paul Keating managed a rock band. You do have to be a lawyer to become attorney-general, but you don't have to be an economist to be the prime minister. Indeed, you don't even have to be an economist to be the treasurer.

Although most politicians have no training in economics, and sometimes lack even the most superficial knowledge of how the Australian economy works, they are often highly skilled in using economic language to bamboozle or silence the public. They use words like *productivity* when they mean *profit*. They say things like 'The economy is overheated' when they mean 'I don't think we should increase the minimum wage'. And they say things like 'We need to balance the needs of the economy and the health risks to our population' when they mean 'I would be happy to see more people die if we can boost the profits of the retail and tourism industries'. Words matter.

Economics is far more complicated than political slogans such as 'Jobs and growth' suggest. Until recently, conservative politicians in Australia argued that budget deficits were proof of poor economic management. For example, Tony Abbott was elected in 2013 on a promise to fix what he called a 'budget emergency', and Josh Frydenberg declared in April 2019 that the Commonwealth budget was 'back in the black' – but after six Coalition[1] deficits in a row, COVID-19 hit and they delivered the biggest budget deficit in modern Australian history and (rightly) said it was no big deal. The power of econobabble is such that the Coalition still claim to have some unique skill in managing the economy despite failing spectacularly according to their own (baseless) criteria.

Questions such as 'Should we have a deficit or shouldn't we?' and 'If we are going to have a deficit, what should we be spending more money on?' don't have simple answers. And most importantly, economics is no better placed to tell the public what we should, or shouldn't, be spending money on than it is capable of predicting what will happen to the economy next year. As the famous economist

J.K. Galbraith once said, 'The only function of economic forecasting is to make astrology look respectable.'

But despite the demonstrated inability of economists, Coalition politicians or indeed anyone to make accurate predictions about what will happen to the economy with and without certain policies, our elected representatives continue to spend a mountain of public money buying such forecasts and models. They might as well seed clouds or buy lottery tickets.

Catholic priests used to say mass in Latin, knowing full well that their mostly uneducated audiences had little idea what was being said. But the purpose of such sermons was not to explain or persuade. The purpose was to silence. How can you disagree with something you don't understand?

Economists often speak in Latin and Ancient Greek. We love to wear folk down with a few *deltas* and *gammas*, before finishing them off with a bit of *ceteris paribus*. One of our other good tricks is to use words that sound like English but which have very specific meanings in the field of economics. We use simple-sounding words like *efficiency* and *unemployment* to draw the unsuspecting in. Then, when they admit to thinking that unemployment is measured by the number of people on the dole (it's not), or to thinking that efficiency means reducing waste (not to economists it doesn't), we slam the door on their fingers.

To be clear, I'm not suggesting for a minute that only economists should be allowed to be prime minister or

treasurer, or to run a business. That would be as dangerous as it is undemocratic. My point is that the vast majority
of people who talk confidently about 'what the economy
needs' have no more knowledge of economics than the average citizen. What they possess is confidence, not credentials.

The primary purpose of the econobabble that fills our
airwaves is to keep ordinary Australians out of the big
debates about tax, fairness, climate change and the provision of essential services. Like the congregation at a Latin
mass, they can't follow what the high priests are saying.
And that's just the way politicians and so-called business
leaders like it.

ECONOMICS IS MORE FREQUENTLY USED TO CONCEAL THAN TO REVEAL

Australians are among the richest people to ever live,
and collectively we are far richer now than we were forty
years ago. But such is the power of econobabble that
although we were told how lucky we were that our great
economic managers delivered nearly thirty years of economic growth in a row, we were simultaneously told that
we couldn't afford to have the high-quality public services
that we used to have. It gets better: when the economy was
growing strongly in the 1990s and 2000s, we were told that
we 'couldn't afford' to spend more public money on policies like free childcare, but when the economy collapsed

during the COVID-19 crisis we suddenly could afford it! I told you econobabble was powerful.

But while econobabble is a great way to conceal the options we really face, and the real motivations for the choices our elected representatives make, it is a terrible way to have a constructive, inclusive public debate about options, priorities and trade-offs. What it does do well is stifle debate, and confound and confuse Australians. That's the reason we hear so much of it.

Like any discipline, economics has its own professional language – jargon – which can be used either to speed up conversations between experts or to keep the uninitiated out of their deliberations. When non-economist politicians use economic jargon while talking to non-economist voters, you can be pretty certain what their objective is.

Just as a patient having a heart attack in an emergency ward is unlikely to understand what the doctors are saying to each other, so too someone listening to two economists argue about the shape of the yield curve and the likely effectiveness of monetary policy will miss the significance of much of what is said. But once the crisis has passed, a good doctor also knows how to use an entirely different vocabulary to explain to the patient what happened, what was done about it, and what it all means for the patient's future.

Anyone who really understands their subject matter can explain it to someone else. *If* they really understand it. And *if* they really want the other person to understand it too.

Like economics itself, jargon isn't dangerous. But econobabble is used to limit the menu of democratic choices that we are offered. Politicians rely on it to make themselves seem smart and to make the public feel dumb. In recent decades, the strategy has worked a treat in convincing the majority of the population to accept inherently unpopular policies like privatisation and tax cuts for the very wealthy, but it has clearly been far less successful in delivering low unemployment, high-quality services or solutions to problems like climate change.

WHAT THE HELL IS THE HANG SENG?

If elected leaders are to tackle big problems on our behalf, we need them to identify those problems clearly, explain the different options for fixing them, and build a case for their preferred response. It's simple stuff, and it is the opposite of relying on econobabble to conceal problems, options and consequences.

But it is not just the politicians who need to change. Policy advocates, the media and the voting public all have to admit some simple truths. Let's start with an easy one: almost no one knows what the Hang Seng Index is.

The Hang Seng is an indicator of the financial performance of the companies listed on Hong Kong's stock exchange, which is Asia's third-largest. Almost no Australians know that, or care. And we can be pretty sure that anyone who does actually know about such things will not be tuning in to the nightly television news to find out what happened to their investments that day. So why do television stations waste their time on such indicators each night?

Presumably for the same reason that economists speak in Latin. The Hang Seng – and other similar indexes, such as the ASX 200, the Nikkei and the Dow Jones – are there to remind us every night that there is much we don't understand. Its role is to silence, not to inform. There is nothing to stop our news broadcasters from providing nightly updates on inequality, hospital waiting lists, greenhouse gas emissions or childhood obesity rates. But instead of providing Australians with a regular flow of information that they care about, they bombard people with data they neither care about nor understand. It's an old trick, but it works.

MARKETS DON'T HAVE FEELINGS – RICH PEOPLE HAVE FEELINGS

The overwhelming majority of Australians think that we should spend more money on health, education and public transport. The vast majority of us also believe that Apple, Google and Gina Rinehart should pay more tax.[2] Nearly everyone agrees that big corporations should be banned from donating money to political parties,[3] and that the federal government should create an anti-corruption watchdog.[4] We live in a democracy, yet the fact that most of us want these changes is not sufficient to achieve them. 'Business leaders' tell us that we can only consider such changes after we 'consult the markets', or after we get the budget into surplus, or . . . just not now.

The high priests of econobabble often tell us that 'the markets', like the gods of cultures past, can be angry. They can be vengeful. And they can punish nonbelievers. We must consult them cautiously. Tony Abbott once supported holding an inquiry into the impact of mining companies' decisions to double their iron ore production on the price of iron ore. However, a week later, after pressure from those same mining companies, he told us that to even inquire into the fall in the iron ore price might spook the markets, and stated that 'the last thing this government would ever want to do is interfere with a free market like the iron ore market'. Especially after the mining companies tell us not to, it seems.[5]

The government was similarly deferential on the issue of a royal commission into the behaviour of our big banks. Right up until the big banks themselves wrote to Malcolm Turnbull suggesting he should hold a royal commission into their failings, the then prime minister and his whole front bench were adamant that to merely inquire into the banks would invite the wrath of 'the markets'. In the words of the then treasurer, Scott Morrison, the calls for a royal commission were 'nothing more than crass populism seeking to undermine confidence in the banking system, which is the key to jobs and growth in this country'.

As it turned out, the big banks were guilty of stealing from dead people, exploiting intellectually disabled people and failing to meet their obligations to detect money laundering. While the process was excruciating for a large number of bankers and regulators, the sky didn't fall in and the economy was not ruined. While bank shareholders might have been angry, the financial markets coped effortlessly with the damning findings of Justice Hayne.

While markets are real, it is absurd to suggest that they have 'feelings', 'needs' or 'demands'. Markets are a place where buyers and sellers of a product come together. It might be a physical place like a fish market, or a virtual place like eBay or a stock exchange. But regardless of their form, markets never have feelings. Ever.

Rich people, on the other hand, do have feelings. And rich people who own billions of dollars' worth of shares in a company often have very strong feelings. They have feelings about government policies, and they have feelings about tax rates.

But the feelings of rich people are quite different to the 'feelings' of the market. Consider the following example, which shows how effectively economic language can conceal what's actually going on. Both the following reports describe the same event:

Markets reacted angrily today to news the government is considering tightening thin capitalisation provisions, which have provided foreign investors with strong incentives to expand their Australian operations.

Rich foreigners reacted angrily today at news that they might have to pay tax on the profits they earn in Australia. After the government announced that it was considering clamping down on some of the most lucrative forms of multinational profit-shifting, some very wealthy Americans threatened to take their businesses away from Australia if they were forced to pay tax.

Words matter.

Here's another one. Let's replace the words 'the economy' with 'rich people's yacht money':

Sure, we could invest a lot of public money in renewable energy, but think about what that would do to rich people's yacht money.

Yes, Australia could spend as much on health and education as Norway and Sweden, but have you considered what that would do to rich people's yacht money?

The reason we have to cut taxes is that it will be good for rich people's yacht money.

Governments and citizens should be concerned about the impact of changes in government policy on businesses, employment and the distribution of income. But the notion that Australia, one of the richest countries the world has ever known, can't change its laws without consulting with 'the market' is as absurd as it is alarming. In effect, we are regularly being told by our own leaders that Australia can't change its laws unless some very rich people, most of whom live in other countries, say it's okay for us to do so.

The trick only works when, like a monster in a horror movie, 'the market' seems close enough to be threatening but not so close that we can see it is made of papier-mâché. The vague, lurking but formless presence of 'the market' is far more ominous than reports about what happened to the weighted average price of shares in South-East Asian stock exchanges today (AKA the Hang Seng).

The nightly news gives us a regular reminder that 'the market' is watching and judging us. It might seem common sense that if we collected more tax, as they do in Norway, we could have health and education systems just as good as Norwegians have. But econobabble limits the options in front of us. 'What? You want to spend more money on health and education? Just imagine how the market would react to such a suggestion! You must be mad! You must not understand economics!'

Of course, in reality the market doesn't *want* anything. The market doesn't judge us, or anybody. The market is a metaphor, and it can no more judge our actions than Zeus or Apollo. The really scary question is whether or not the people going on about 'market sentiment' know this. As the saying goes, the best patsy doesn't know they are a patsy.

Whether the econobabblers are talking about 'what the markets want' or 'what the economy needs' or what a 'responsible government must do', their language and metaphors are systematically used to limit the range of options that are 'sensible' or 'pragmatic' or (most frequently) 'responsible'. Consider the following statements, both of which convey the same economic information:

- The budget deficit has grown rapidly in the last three years, even as the economy has grown strongly.

- Over the last three years, the government has invested heavily in the new infrastructure that rapid economic growth requires.

Just as there is nothing 'irresponsible' or 'unsustainable' about an individual borrowing to buy a house, or a company borrowing to invest in a profitable new project, there is nothing irresponsible about a government borrowing to invest in the infrastructure that a rapidly growing population and economy need.

But for someone who would prefer to see governments collect less tax from him or herself and spend less money on others, droning on about the way that taxes are a 'burden' that 'destroy incentive' or about how welfare payments 'discourage work' sounds a lot less selfish, and is far more effective politically, than stating the simple truth. As J.K. Galbraith once said, 'The modern conservative is engaged in one of man's oldest exercises in moral philosophy; that is, the search for a superior moral justification for selfishness.'

YOUR MONEY OR YOUR LIFE?

'Money has never made man happy, nor will it, there is nothing in its nature to produce happiness. The more of it one has, the more one wants.'
—Benjamin Franklin, co-author of the US Constitution

How much should other Australians spend to protect your life? Or your partner's life? Or some stranger's life? Economists have no idea what the right answers to those questions are, and most Australians respond differently depending on how we ask the question. When twelve young Thai boys were trapped inside a cave and threatened by rising flood waters, the world mobilised to save their lives. No resources, we were told, were spared. But when it comes to providing subsidies for new medicines or employing more nurses to work in remote communities, we are told that budgets are tight and hard decisions must be made.

When it comes to COVID-19, how much should we be willing to spend to protect 25 million people from the risk of infection? Should we 'let it rip' like they have in the United States, or should we 'shut the economy down'? And who should make this decision? While there's been lots of econobabble spoken about the policy response to COVID-19, as we will discuss in the following chapters, there is nothing in the economics textbooks that suggests that economists are uniquely positioned to advise on how much death and physical suffering equates to a year spent enduring unemployment.

Over the next ten years, the Morrison government expects to spend more than $270 billion on defence, including $9.3 billion to develop new hypersonic weapons, $5 billion for a new undersea surveillance network, and $7 billion for new space-based defence capabilities. While that is more than the direct budgetary costs of responding to the 'once in a century' pandemic of COVID-19, there has been relatively little public or political debate about the relative cost of defending Australians from a health emergency compared to the cost of buying submarines or fighter aircraft.

When it comes to avoiding deaths, some lives have always been more important than others. Consider, for example, the fact that state governments are willing to spend large amounts of money attempting to reduce the risk of shark attacks, when there are clear shortages of proven life-saving devices, such as dialysis machines, in remote Indigenous communities.[6] Similarly, although far more people die from drowning than shark attacks, there is little political incentive to regulate swimming.

Of course, it's not all about money. While there has been significant outrage, particularly from the conservative commentariat, at the inconvenience associated with mandatory mask-wearing to reduce the spread of COVID-19, the fact that over twenty years Australians have given up an enormous number of legal rights in the 'fight against terrorism', lockdowns and border closures has attracted far less attention.

There is no 'right' way to decide which risks we should defend ourselves against and which ones we should let rip, but the 'economic rationalists' who for decades have argued that we need to make decisions with our heads rather than our hearts are remarkably silent when it comes to comparing our approach to defence spending and our approach to climate change. Defence spending gets a free pass, even though no one believes for a second that any amount would protect us from an attack by a motivated superpower. When it comes to finding solutions to climate change, we are told that Australia acting alone is pointless, and yet when it comes to defence spending we are told (if we are told anything) that we have a moral obligation to 'play our part'. As with all government decisions, there's no right way to make them, but those who make them should be able to explain themselves. Shouldn't they?

But back to COVID-19. It's one thing to debate how we should treat the threat of COVID compared to how we treat the threat of invasion, the threat of terrorism or the threat of climate change, but COVID has highlighted a much bigger problem with our public debate: we don't know what our goal is.

For decades we have been told that if we grow the economy enough (measured in terms of GDP), we will be rich enough to have all the things we want, like good education, good health and a clean environment. But when COVID-19 hit, the Australian public was confronted with a brutal truth that had previously been kept politely hidden: powerful people are willing to sacrifice Australians in order to grow the economy.

The ideas that if we grow the economy we can afford to help everyone, and that if we sacrifice some people now we can all be richer in the future, are, of course, two sides of the same coin. But for decades the public only saw the shiny side: be patient, make sacrifices today, and we will all be better off tomorrow. But when COVID-19 struck, the dull side of the coin was in full view: if we let COVID spread through our community, it will kill tens of thousands but those of us who survive will be better off in the end.

Again, there is no right answer to such questions. While it is not polite to admit it, nation-states make decisions about life and death all the time. Australia conscripted soldiers who were killed on the Kokoda Trail and in the Vietnam War; the Commonwealth government allowed nuclear testing in South Australia on lands that were still used by Indigenous people; we had the death penalty until 1985; the Australian Navy has turned back refugee boats at sea; and the Australian Federal Police has shared intelligence on more than 1500 Australians suspected of drug trafficking with countries where such crimes carry the death penalty.[7] So we should not be surprised that some 'hard heads' were of the view that the 'best' response to COVID-19 was to let it kill as many people as it would, hopefully as quickly as possible, so that we could 'get back to normal' as quickly as possible.

It reminds me of an argument made by a former chief of staff of the US Air Force, four-star general Curtis LeMay: 'I think there are many times when it would be most efficient to use nuclear weapons. However, the public . . . in this country and throughout the world throw up their hands in horror when you mention nuclear weapons, just because of the propaganda that's been fed to them.'[8]

Countries kill people when they declare war, decide which drugs to subsidise and set the budget for preventive health measures such as skin cancer and breast cancer screening. Sometimes we can identify the specific individuals that die, and sometimes they simply show up in the population statistics, but regardless, there is no doubt that policy decisions cost and save. Just as surely as the US approach to gun ownership costs lives, the US approach to managing COVID-19 has cost lives as well.

While we will never know how many Australians might have died from COVID-19 if we had 'let it rip' rather than shut our international borders, many local borders and hundreds of thousands of businesses, what we do know is that, as of January 2021, if the same proportion of Australians had died of COVID-19 as had died in the United States, then the Australian death toll would have been over 29,000. At the time of writing, fewer than 1000 Australians had died.

So how much are those lives 'worth'? What reduction in GDP should we be willing to incur to save 28,000 lives? And who should make such a decision? Economists can offer some crude tools to help weigh up the options:

- We can suggest that we survey people and ask them what their life is worth, but we know full well that if we ask them what a stranger's life is worth, we will get a radically different answer.

- We can assume that each person's life is 'worth' their expected lifetime income – but do we really believe that the life of a full-time financial planner is worth twice as much as that of a part-time teacher?

- We can assume that each life in Australia is worth the same amount, and that that amount is best estimated by average GDP per person – but do we really think that the life of an infant and of a retiree are identical in value?

- We can 'weight' lives by age in order to focus on the 'years of life saved' rather than the number of individuals saved – but again, do we really believe that the life of an infant is worth ten or twenty times more than a grandparent's? And who decides if it is ten times, or twenty time, or 13.2 times?

- Finally, how many foreigners' lives is an Australian life worth? If they come from a higher-income country than ours, are they worth more? If they are residents in our country but not citizens, are they worth less?

In multiple opinion polls, the overwhelming majority of the Australian public have expressed support for the decision to put the protection of human life ahead of the maximisation of the size of the economy. But while these views have been overwhelmingly popular, including at the ballot box, they are by no means unanimous. Significantly for the themes explored in this book, the majority of trained economists who have been asked whether governments should prioritise human or economic health have favoured the protection of life.

While it is not wrong for people to admit to preferring personal freedom to public health, a personal preference of this sort has nothing to do with economics – which of course makes it a perfect subject to econobabble about.

HOW TO DECODE ECONOBABBLE

There are four simple rules you can use to decode the jargon that politicians and businesspeople so frequently use to keep the public out of the public debate:

- Ask them to say it again in English. If they know what they are talking about, that won't be hard.

- Listen carefully, and get them to clarify what key words mean to them (for instance, the meaning of a word like *efficiency* often varies greatly depending on who's using it). Again, people who know what they are talking about and have nothing to hide won't mind explaining what they mean by terms like *efficiency* or *competitive*.

- Ask them if their strong opinions about how parts of the economy work are based on evidence or simply 'gut feel'. It's one thing to 'know' that tax cuts will make rich people work harder and thus increase the incomes of poor people, but it's another thing altogether to have evidence. (Hint: some of the richest countries in the world with the lowest unemployment have high taxes. Northern Europe does exist.)

- Walk away when they start talking in generalities about 'supply and demand' or 'market forces'. Blaming 'the law of demand' for an economic outcome is like blaming the law of gravity for a plane crash – it's proof that the speaker has no idea what they are talking about, or no intention of explaining their thinking to you.

Too often we have allowed ourselves to be spoken down to by those who seek to serve us. It's time we demanded better. In the following chapters we'll look at a number of important policy areas in which econobabble is used to avoid democratic debate: climate change, unemployment, debt and the budget, the free market and free trade. We'll also look at the business of economic modelling, and how it's regularly used to deceive.

In this second edition of this book, we will also take a look at the language used to describe the value of life and death, particularly in relation to policies to protect us from COVID-19. And we'll take a closer look at the debate around public debt in the context of the enormous budget deficits delivered by Australia's federal Coalition government. Finally, we'll consider what can be done to fix our debate about the economy – even if we can't agree on how to fix the economy itself.

My hope is that this book will empower you to call out the bullshit when you hear it – because democracy just can't cope with too much BS.

2.

Tackling Climate Change

I t takes a flood of econobabble to convince people that it would be cheaper and better to cause climate change than to prevent it. But a flood we have had.

The same mining companies that are planning to shed tens of thousands of mining jobs by introducing robot trucks and trains spend tens of millions of dollars per year lobbying against ambitious climate policy on the basis that, you guessed it, we need to protect jobs. And the media takes them seriously!

Not since menthol cigarettes were marketed as a 'healthy option' has an industry been so audacious in its hypocrisy. When the coal industry in the Hunter Valley switched from underground mining to open-pit mining, it shed 20,000 jobs. When the Kennett government privatised Victoria's electricity generators, the new owners shed 10,000 jobs.[1] But when an overwhelming majority of the population want to transition away from fossil fuels, the econobabblers pretend that mining jobs are sacrosanct.

Sitting just behind the ridiculous claim that causing climate change is a good idea because it creates jobs is plenty of econobabble. Terms such as *least cost abatement, discount rate, abatement cost curve* and *network stability* help industry lobbyists make the inexplicable seen inevitable.

A millennium's worth of common sense that 'an ounce of prevention is better than a pound of cure' and that 'a stitch in time saves nine' has somehow been transformed into the modern conventional wisdom: 'Let's just let things rip and assume that, in the future, someone will invent a solution for the problems we're causing.' The fact that people who call themselves 'conservatives' are driving this radical new approach to risk makes their rhetorical and political achievement all the more remarkable.

The biggest and most cynical hoax of modern political life is the assertion that tackling climate change will be 'expensive' and 'harmful to the economy'. On the contrary, it will save us a lot of money in the short term, and will save us from permanently altering the climate in the long run. It won't 'hurt the economy' or 'upset the markets', but it will harm the parts of the economy that sell carbon pollution, and it will hurt the people with lots of money invested in those industries. Just as the transition from horses to cars was bad for people who bred horses and great for people who made cars, the transition from coal and oil to renewables and batteries means there will be winners and losers. But the fact that the coal industry will shrink if we tackle climate change does not prove that tackling climate change is bad for the economy, any more than suggesting that the shift away from whale oil, asbestos or photographic film was 'bad for the economy'.

The truth is that tackling climate change won't 'cost jobs' in any economy-wide sense. Investment in new technologies creates jobs in the short term, and increases productivity in the long term.

Some fossil-fuel billionaires have spent decades, and a lot of money, telling us that dealing with climate change will hurt the poor, and, more bizarrely, that causing climate change is a good way to help the poor. It's not the fact that these people would lie to protect their interests that is surprising – it's that anyone else, especially our elected representatives and media, takes their self-serving nonsense seriously.

While Scott Morrison famously waved a lump of coal around in parliament, Malcolm Turnbull once claimed that blocking the construction of Adani's enormous Carmichael mine in Queensland's Galilee Basin would not make 'one iota' of difference to global greenhouse gas emissions, yet he simultaneously claimed that blocking the same mine would prevent poor people in developing countries from gaining access to affordable energy.[2] Let's break that claim down into its component parts.

The first part of the then prime minister's claim – that building new supply capacity in Australia has no impact on global supply and global consumption – makes no economic sense. First-year economics tells us that building new mines increases the supply of coal, pushes down the price and, in turn, leads to an increase in the quantity consumed. And it's not just the economic textbooks that predict this sequence of events. Ivan Glasenberg, the former CEO of Glencore, the world's largest coal trading company, has repeatedly made the same observation.[3]

But let's assume that Turnbull was right when he suggested that building new coal mines wouldn't lead to an increase in the amount of coal supplied. If that were the case, and new coal production in Australia simply displaced coal production in another country, then how could building new mines help to provide the additional energy required to lift millions of people out of energy poverty?

While logic dictates that Australian coal could *either* displace overseas coal production *or* add to world production to help lift poor people out of 'energy poverty', econobabble allows Australian coal production to do both at the same time!

Econobabble is a powerful tool, especially when used by the rich and powerful – but as we will discuss in the final chapter, econobabblers have a weak spot: they are vulnerable to the demand for simple answers to simple questions.

BLACK IS WHITE, UP IS DOWN AND THE MAIN GOAL OF MINING COMPANIES IS TO HELP THE POOR

The climate change debate is not a fight about science – it is a fight about economics and politics. There aren't many 'climate sceptics' in countries that don't have large fossil-fuel industries. Boris Johnson, Angela Merkel and Arnold Schwarzenegger aren't considered 'left wing' in their home countries on the basis that they accept the science of climate change. And the Australian media don't take fluoride sceptics or vaccination sceptics seriously – but there isn't a lot of money to be made out of bad teeth and sick kids.

'Climate sceptics' and the economic 'experts' who back them up have a few favoured talking points:

- Doing something about climate change would cost thousands of jobs.

- We can't afford schools and hospitals without all the tax paid by the mining industry.

- A carbon tax would destroy our exports and ruin our economy.

- Because the sun doesn't always shine and the wind doesn't always blow, we can't rely on renewable energy.

Fossil-fuel companies and their lobbyists trot out these arguments at every opportunity in order to justify ignoring the findings of the world's scientific community. In this chapter we will take each argument in turn. But before we decode the econobabble used by the polluters, we should understand a few important truths.

SUBSIDIES CAUSE CLIMATE CHANGE, AND REMOVING THEM WOULD SAVE GOVERNMENTS A FORTUNE

Climate change is primarily caused by the burning of fossil fuels, and coal is the single biggest source of greenhouse gas emissions in the world.[4] All the coal mined in Australia is heavily subsidised by governments. Indeed, governments around the world, over the past century, have spent hundreds of billions of taxpayer dollars supporting the construction of coal mines, coal-fired power stations, and the ports and railways needed to transport coal. Taxpayers even paid for the very long, expensive and inefficient power lines that connect remote power stations to cities, where most of the energy is used. The former federal resources minister Senator Matt Canavan even defended calls to subsidise the Adani coal mine in Queensland on the basis that every other coal mine in Australia had been subsidised, declaring: 'The development of almost every minerals province in Australia has involved government investment. The exception is the Pilbara, but the private rail lines that criss-cross there would be less than ideal for the cattle sector in North Queensland.'[5]

Attending a public school in Australia is cheap because the state and federal governments pick up most of the costs, and the same is true for 'cheap' coal. According to the Queensland budget papers, between 2008–09 and 2013–14 the taxpayers of that state spent $9.5 billion to build infrastructure needed by the coal mining industry.[6] While the industry argues that taxpayer-provided coal loaders aren't a subsidy, the Queensland Treasury disagrees: 'Governments face budget constraints, and spending on mining-related infrastructure means less infrastructure spending in other areas, including social infrastructure such as hospitals and schools.'[7]

Everyone knows that 'coal is cheap', but few realise it is so cheap because of all the government support it has received over the past century. Imagine if you approached the government and proposed that you would build a hotel in a beautiful remote location. 'Foreign tourists will love it,' you say, 'and it will create jobs for the local Indigenous population. All I need is for the government to build me a port, an airport, an access road, an electricity supply, a water supply and a sewerage treatment works.' Having convinced the government to do all that, imagine that you were then able to persuade the public that you hadn't received any subsidies at all! Econobabble is a powerful tool.

Of course, it's not just coal that Australian governments like to to subsidise. While there has been global discussion of the benefits of kick-starting the post-COVID economy with 'Green New Deal' spending measures, here in Australia the prime minister has focused on the potential for a 'gas-led recovery'. Having appointed gas executives to lead his National COVID-19 Commission Advisory Board,[8] Scott Morrison has subsequently announced his support for billions of dollars in public funding for privately owned gas infrastructure.[9]

And then there are trucks. While ordinary motorists pay 42.3 cents per litre in fuel excise, heavy vehicles pay only 25.8 cents per litre. And while fuel excise is indexed to inflation, it is the transport minister who decides whether to increase the heavy vehicle user charge – and for the last few years he has decided not to increase it at all.[10] Despite the fact that a single big truck can do up to 20,000 times as much damage to the road as a car, trucks pay a lower rate of fuel tax than passenger vehicles.

Subsidies are an important policy tool. We subsidise vaccinations, public schools and public transport because we want to encourage their use. And we tax cigarettes and alcohol because we want to discourage their use. The fact that we are subsidising new coal mines, new gas infrastructure and heavy vehicle use provides clear evidence of our elected representatives' real motivations. Money speaks more clearly than econobabble, and it's clear that Australian governments want more mines, more gas, and for freight transport to shift from rail to road. That's why our contribution to climate change is getting worse – our policies are designed to deliver that outcome, while our public debate is designed to conceal it.

WOULD YOU LIKE FREE COAL WITH THAT?

It gets worse. It's not just money that we use to subsidise the fossil-fuel industry, it's real resources as well. While car companies have to buy the steel they need to make cars, and bakers have to buy the flour they need to make bread, coal miners sometimes get 'their' coal for free. A decision by a government to give free coal to coal miners might be a bit hard to explain, and that's where econobabble comes in.

In order to 'encourage' (subsidise) the construction of new coal mines in Queensland's Galilee Basin, the former LNP state government led by Campbell Newman proposed a 'royalty ramp-up' or a 'royalty holiday' for the mines. While the subsequent Labor government led by Annastacia Palaszczuk initially ruled out providing any such subsidy, it later relented and allowed Adani to delay royalty payments for at least five years – a deal worth an estimated $271 million.[11]

How nice! Who wouldn't want a holiday in Queensland? But what does it actually mean?

Royalties are the price that miners pay for the resources they take from the ground. The term relates to the fact that the Crown (or the Queen's governments, in Australian states) owns the minerals our nation's land contains. In *The Beverly Hillbillies*, the Clampett family profited from the oil they discovered on their land, but in Australia it's the state, not the landholder, that is supposed to get rich from our underground wealth. At least, that's the theory.

While the details of both Campbell Newman's and Annastacia Palaszczuk's offers to the Galilee coal miners were declared 'commercial-in-confidence', what is crystal clear is that state and federal governments don't offer subsidised loans to help bakers pay for flour, cafes pay for coffee beans or hotels pay for beds and curtains. For reasons which econobabble helps to keep unclear, Australian governments just like to help some industries with cash subsidies and subsidised loans.

Of course, the miners say that a royalty holiday isn't a subsidy. But if a government gave them free rent for their headquarters in Brisbane, that would be a subsidy. And if we gave them free electricity or free water, that would be a subsidy too. But apparently giving them low-interest loans isn't a subsidy – it's an 'investment'. The ultimate irony of all of the subsidies we provide the fossil-fuel industry is that, on the one hand, they claim to be the backbone of the economy and the budget, but at the same time they argue that without subsidies their projects can't possibly go ahead. So which is it? The role of econobabble is not just to provide dodgy answers to such questions, but to prevent them from being asked in the first place.

The willingness of governments – not just recently, and not just in Australia – to use taxpayers' money to 'develop' the coal industry, and then, having done so, to give the coal away for free or at heavily discounted prices, is one of the major reasons that coal is considered to be such a 'cheap' form of energy. Cars would be cheap if taxpayers paid for the car factories and gave car companies free steel. And bread would be cheap if taxpayers funded bread factories and gave the bakers free wheat. Likewise renewables. Australia is a rich country, and we can subsidise any industry we want – the question is, why do we like subsidising fossil fuels so much?

The conservative governments that love subsidising the mining industry have typically raged against the provision of subsidies to the textile, automotive and other industries. Hypocrisy on such a scale can only survive under a thick coating of econobabble.

BUT WITHOUT SUBSIDIES AND FREE INFRASTRUCTURE, FOSSIL-FUEL PROJECTS WON'T GO AHEAD!

Exactly.

In recent decades, those seeking to respond to the scientific warnings about the catastrophic consequences of climate change have expended enormous personal and political energy pushing for carbon taxes and emissions trading schemes. And there is no doubt these policies are sensible and potentially beneficial. But what is unclear is why the strategists behind the global push for climate action focused so much effort on the hard task of introducing a new tax and so little on the historically easier task of opposing taxpayer subsidies for unpopular industries.

The fossil-fuel industry is adamant that it wouldn't or couldn't mine as much coal or drill as much gas without the enormous taxpayer support it receives. That's great to know. If the miners and drillers are telling the truth about this, then Australia can significantly reduce its greenhouse gas emissions by doing nothing more than ending its fossil-fuel subsidies. And the money which is saved can be spent on health and education – areas that voters want to be funded better. That doesn't sound too scary or too economically harmful, does it?

But what if the miners and drillers are lying, and ending the subsidies doesn't stop them from mining at all? Well, if that's the case, then why should governments continue giving them billions of dollars? If we scrap the subsidies and the miners keep mining and the drillers keep drilling, then our governments can still spend the spare tens of billions of dollars on health and education – or perhaps on non-polluting forms of energy production such as solar or wind.

Put simply, it takes a lot of taxpayer money to make fossil fuels 'cheap'. Removing the infrastructure subsidies to miners will save taxpayers a fortune. Ensuring fossil-fuel companies pay a fair royalty for the resources they take from our ground will raise another fortune. And if the result of filling the government's coffers with all of that money is an increase in coal and gas prices and a reduction in coal consumption . . . well, that's even better.

But instead of removing subsidies, the Morrison government is considering new ones, with the National COVID-19 Commission Advisory Board – the one led by a gas industry veteran – proposing up to $6 billion worth of public spending on the gas industry.[12] Again, the economics of subsidies is simple: they work. The hard question isn't an economic one, though, but a democratic one: which industries do we want to grow, and which ones do we want to shrink?

ECONOMISTS AREN'T THE ONLY ONES WHO MAKE SIMPLISTIC ASSUMPTIONS

Courses in introductory economics rely on a highly simplified concept known as 'perfect competition'. In the imaginary world of perfect competition, there are lots of small producers who trade with lots of customers, no one has any market power, consumers are rational, sellers are honest, and there are no advantages from mass production (or *economies of scale*, if you want to sound like an economist). And get this: in perfect competition, no firm can make big profits! So whenever you see a company making billions in profits, you know you are looking at a company that isn't operating in the kind of highly competitive industry the simple economic models assume.

It makes sense to start teaching economics with a simplified model like this. But it doesn't make sense to apply it to real-world problems. Yet this is what many economists and policy-makers do when they try to force a complex reality to fit a simple model. To a man with a hammer, as they say, the whole world looks like a nail.

Unfortunately, most environmentalists, scientists and politicians who advocate for better climate policy have made a similar error: they have assumed that the market for coal is working relatively well, and that it only suffers from one 'market failure' in the form of the pollution costs that are ignored by miners and by power station owners. (If you refer to pollution as *external costs* or *externalities*, you can really start to sound like an economist.)

If the market for coal was 'perfectly competitive', then there would be no price distortions, no market power and no subsidies, and introducing a carbon price would be a logical policy if we wanted to reduce the pollution that cause climate change. But of course the coal market isn't perfectly competitive – not by a long shot. So while theory might say that introducing a carbon price is the best way to reform the industry and reduce pollution, in reality eliminating subsidies makes more economic sense (and far more political sense).

Unfortunately, too many environmentalists and economists have failed to recognise that the coal industry is so heavily subsidised. Their idealistic view of the coal market has meant that, rather than focusing on the subsidies given to coal mines, oil exploration and coal-fired electricity generators, they have tried to educate the population about science and build support for a new tax. Science is hard and taxes are rarely popular, and so the strategy hasn't worked very well so far.

The reason the mining industry is fighting so hard to deny that it is heavily subsidised proves the importance of removing its subsidies. In a perfectly competitive world a carbon tax makes a lot of sense, but in the messy world we have created for ourselves, abolishing the subsidies the miners rely on is not only the most efficient way to start tackling climate change, it will also be the cheapest and the most popular.

DECODING THE ECONOBABBLE USED TO SUPPORT CLIMATE INACTION

The best way to win an argument with the polluters is to highlight the internal contradictions in their arguments. The coal miners say they can't live without subsidies, while the political conservatives say they don't believe in giving out subsidies, so it shouldn't be hard to win such a fight. But it is. People with billions of dollars invested in pollution-causing industries are not going to walk away from our money without a battle.

The first thing we should understand is that the polluters themselves do not believe the arguments they use to support their industry. The polluters have spent a lot of time and money testing and developing arguments that are designed to be persuasive, or at least challenging, for progressive and centrist voters. That's why companies that want to abolish unfair-dismissal laws always say they are worried about 'protecting jobs', and why those who want to profit from causing climate change argue that environmentalists don't care about the poor.

Let's take a closer look at their main arguments.

I. Doing something about climate change would cost thousands of jobs.

That's correct – it will. All significant change results in some workers and capitalists losing out, and change is the only constant in our economy. Ending the whaling industry cost whalers their jobs. Ending asbestos mining cost asbestos workers their jobs. The invention of the digital camera destroyed the jobs of photo development lab workers.

According to the Australian Bureau of Statistics, an average of around 330,000 people get new jobs each month in Australia – that's more than six times the total number of people employed in coal mining in Australia.[13] But the fact that so many new jobs get created each month doesn't mean that the number of employed people grow that much each month, because lots of people quit or lose their jobs each month as well. In short, the labour market is more like a swirling river than a still pond, and people change their jobs all the time, despite the enormous personal, family, community, social and economic costs.

The sick joke, however, is that the industries and political parties making the most noise about 'protecting jobs' from policies that aim to tackle climate change are the same voices who want to make it easier for companies to sack workers, and harder for the unemployed to get unemployment benefits. Even in the midst of the pandemic-induced recession, the Morrison government refused to permanently increase the miserably low unemployment benefit by a significant amount.

Involuntary job losses are devastating, but it is clear that whether or not we tackle climate change, there will be an enormous number of involuntary job losses. Thirty years ago, manufacturing accounted for 17 per cent of employment in Australia. Today, it is 8 per cent. One hundred and ten years ago, agriculture accounted for about 30 per cent of employment in Australia. Today, it is 3 per cent. The conservative commentators who feign concern about jobs in mining rarely mourn the loss of manufacturing jobs.[14] Indeed, when he was treasurer, Joe Hockey taunted the Australian car industry to leave our shores. It did.[15]

Tony Abbott's 2013 declaration that, if elected to government, he would cut 20,000 jobs from the public sector is clear proof that some jobs are less important than others.[16] But if jobs in the public sector are the least important (to politicians talking about jobs, at least), then the coal mining industry must take the biscuit for having the most politically important jobs. How else could an industry that employs only around 52,100 of the 13.8 million employed people in Australia be seen as the backbone of the economy?[17]

While it's true that the 52,000 people who work in coal mining seems large when compared with the 8000 people who work in coal-fired power stations, coal mining is a tiny employer nationally. The manufacturing sector employs 840,700 people, while education employs 1.1 million. Health is the largest single sector, employing 1.75 million.[18]

Even in the small number of regions where most coal mining jobs are concentrated, health is still a larger employer, but you never hear conservative voices talk about how the health sector, or the education sector, are the backbone of regional economies. You also never hear them boasting that capital cities like Sydney and Brisbane employ more people in the mining industry than Far North Queensland, or that, on average, inner-city mining workers get paid more than those who work at the coalface.

In their desperation to pump up the perceived size of the mining industry, lobby groups like the Queensland

Resources Council like to estimate all of the 'indirect' jobs that mining 'creates'. While the use and abuse of these 'job multiplier' effects are discussed in detail in Chapter 7, for now suffice it to say that in the lead-up to the 2020 Queensland election, the QRC claimed that mining was responsible for 46,750 jobs in the inner-city electorate of McConnell; the Queensland Electoral Commission, as it happens, reports that only 39,212 adults live in that electorate.[19] One of them is making shit up.

Building a hospital creates 'indirect jobs' in the construction industry, just like building a mine does. And most nurses spend their wages in the 'local economy', just like most miners do. It's obvious when you stop and think about it, but employment in every industry creates 'indirect jobs' – but not every industry spends tens of millions of dollars paying consultants and taking out full-page ads to make themselves look bigger than they really are.

A former head of the Minerals Council of Australia, Mitch Hooke, told the million-strong audience of the ABC's *Q&A* program in July 2013 that mining was the biggest employer of Indigenous Australians.[20] He meant to say tenth-biggest. Health employs far more Indigenous Australians than mining, but econobabble, backed up by dodgy statistics, rarely goes unchallenged when delivered with confidence by a man wearing an expensive suit.

The coal industry employs less than 1 per cent of employed Australians (0.70 per cent, to be precise[21]), which means that more than 99 per cent of Australians don't work in coal mining. The so-called indirect jobs associated with mining are proportionate to the total employment, which means that mining, at best, creates less than 1 per cent of the 'indirect jobs' in Australia. But hats off to the mining companies: they have spent more money paying economists to exaggerate the size of their industry than any other industry. According to research by the Australia Institute, the PR campaign by the mining industry has been so successful that the average Australian thinks that coal mining employs nearly 10 per cent of the Australian workforce – over ten times more than it does in reality.[22]

Regardless of the tiny size of the coal workforce, any structural change in the economy costs jobs, and any unexpected job loss is traumatic for those concerned, their families and their regions. But the vast majority of people losing jobs in Australia today are not losing them because of climate policy. When Scott Morrison closed our borders to protect Australians from COVID-19, he knew that hundreds of thousands of people in the tourism and education sectors would lose their jobs, and they did. Steam-powered ships destroyed jobs in sail-making, diesel trains destroyed jobs in the stream train business, and smartphones have destroyed hundreds of thousands of jobs in everything from call centres to street directory publishers. Good economic policy doesn't prevent change; it invests in retraining and supporting people. Good social policy gives the unexpectedly unemployed a sense of security and support. It provides them with dignity.

The conservative governments and employer groups that have argued against policies that aim to reduce climate change have done nothing to improve the lot of the unemployed in Australia. In fact, both groups have worked hard to shed tens of thousands of workers from the public sector while arguing it should be harder to get unemployment benefits.

2. We can't afford schools and hospitals without all the tax paid by the mining industry.

'You've got to [decide] whether you want to talk about economically dreamy or economic reality. And the economic reality of Australia is our largest export is fossil fuels, if you want to lose that you've got to be prepared to take a cut down the future for your children's health, your children's education, your grandchildren's education.'
—Barnaby Joyce, former deputy prime minister[23]

The taxes and royalties paid by all mining companies to all levels of government account for around 5 per cent of government revenue.[24] And that's the total amount paid, not the net amount after we deduct the subsidies they receive. In 2020–21 the Queensland government will earn more from speeding fines and car registrations than it does from the coal industry.[25]

These numbers come from state and federal budget papers. There is no 'modelling' or 'interpretation'. Thanks to data released by the ATO, the fact that the mining companies don't pay much tax, and some pay none, is clear for all to see. But a flood of econobabble, and much outright deception, has been effective in concealing this simple truth.

The vast majority of tax revenue collected in Australia comes from the income tax paid by workers, the GST paid by all citizens, and the corporate profit taxes paid by company shareholders. Mining is the backbone of neither our budgets nor our labour market. Indeed, the income tax and GST paid by healthcare and education workers provide more revenue to state and federal governments than the coal mining industry.[26]

According to the Queensland and West Australian Treasuries, the mining industry is a leech that is sucking their states dry.

When pushed to defend the incredible cost to the taxpayer of building their ports, roads and rail lines, the mining industry falls back on claims about 'all the tax' mining companies pay. Leaving aside the fact that, as a proportion of state budgets, the mining industry simply doesn't pay a lot of tax, when taxpayers subsidise the mining industry another problem arises. A big one. The kind of problem that only econobabble can hide. This is what is known as 'opportunity cost'.

One of the first lessons taught in any economics class relates to the foundational economic principle of opportunity cost. Put simply, when a resource is scarce, then whenever that resource is dedicated to one pursuit, the 'opportunity' to use it for something else is lost. For example: your time is finite, and the time you spend reading this book is time you can't spend reading the Queensland budget papers.

Money is another scarce resource for state governments. And so when Queenslanders spend billions of dollars to pay for mining infrastructure, the opportunity to spend that money on hospitals and schools is lost. The same tax dollars can't fund both sectors at the same time.

The Queensland and West Australian Treasuries are adamant that a lot of taxpayer money is spent building infrastructure for the mining industry. The Queensland, West Australian and Commonwealth budget papers make clear that the mining industry doesn't pay a lot of tax. There is simply no truth to the assertion that the mining industry is what pays for our schools and hospitals. None. In fact, the opposite is the case. As the Queensland Treasury itself makes clear, our schools and hospitals are paying a high price for all of the subsidies given to the mining industry.

Such daylight robbery can only occur behind the cloak of econobabble.

3. A carbon tax would destroy our exports and ruin our economy.

> *'The carbon tax will act as a wrecking ball across the economy.'*
>
> —**Tony Abbott**[27]

Tony Abbott's campaign against the carbon tax introduced by Julia Gillard was so destructive that, ten years later, the idea is still politically toxic. The cynicism of the campaign was staggering, with Abbott having himself once advocated a carbon tax. He famously described himself as 'a bit of a weather vane' on climate policy, before arguing that his subsequent opposition to the carbon tax was based on 'principle'.[28]

While it is true that mining accounts for a significant portion of Australia's exports, it's not at all clear whether that is a blessing or a curse. As the mining boom gathered pace from 2004, the value of mining exports increased from $42 billion to $154 billion in 2015.[29] The surge in exports saw Australia's exchange rate with the US dollar soar from US$0.80 to US$1.10. Imported cars became much cheaper, overseas holidays became much cheaper, and many middle-class people decided it was cheaper to get married in Bali or Fiji than in Australia.

Yet at the same time, the manufacturing industry suffered a significant decline, as did the tourism industry. The number of international tourists visiting Far North

Queensland plummeted more than 25 per cent from 865,000 in 2005–06 to 614,000 in 2011–12.[30] Foreign students switched from expensive Australian universities to 'cheaper options' in the United Kingdom and the United States. Agricultural producers had to accept much lower prices for their exports because of the high exchange rate. The devastating impact of a mining boom on other parts of the economy is not unusual. Indeed, it is so well understood and expected that economists have a number of different names for the phenomenon, including the 'Dutch Disease' (after the adverse impact of the Dutch oil discoveries in the North Sea) and the 'resource curse'. But public debate is so broken in Australia that mentioning such evidence provokes criticism for suggesting that mining is anything other than 'the backbone of the economy' (whatever that means), or accusations of wanting to 'shut the mining industry down overnight'. It's not just the climate change and vaccination debates that ignore simple economics.

So were all those extra mining exports good or bad for Australia? The answer, of course, depends on whether you were the Swiss owners of mining giant Glencore, or the Australian owner of a hotel in Cairns. Interestingly, while mining exports grew significantly during the mining boom (no surprise there), the total value of Australian exports as a whole didn't rise significantly as a percentage of GDP. Put simply, the mining exports cannibalised the non-mining exports. Economists use the more polite term *crowding out* to describe this effect, but in short, it's safe to assume that if one major exporter is popping champagne corks, then some other export industry is laying off staff.

All the export data described above is freely available to any politician, journalist or citizen who is willing to go the ABS website. Needless to say, few have taken up the opportunity.

Intriguingly, as the high exchange rate was devastating parts of the tourism and agriculture industries at the height of the mining boom, the peak bodies for those industries were adamant that the opposite was true.[31] Despite the fact that overseas visitors to the Great Barrier Reef collapsed during the mining boom of the mid-2000s, and unemployment rates in Cairns hit 9.2 per cent, the peak tourism body seemed unconcerned that the high exchange rate was harming the industry. Bizarrely, however, as the exchange rate then fell back towards its long-term average, the tourism industry argued that the declining exchange rate was giving it quite a boost![32]

Like so many politicians and journalists, it seems that even the industries that have been directly harmed by the mining boom are either confused by the econobabble or, worse, willing to use econobabble to conceal the need to confront big industries such as mining.

So much for exports – but will a carbon tax destroy the economy?

The people who ran the campaign against the carbon tax were the same people who argue that personal income tax wrecks the economy, that company tax wrecks the economy and, yep, that tax generally wrecks the economy. While there is no doubt that there were mistakes in the way the carbon price was designed and sold to the public, there is also no doubt that the carbon tax package came with very big personal income tax cuts, compensation to households and compensation to industries. It's also true that countries like New Zealand have a carbon price, introduced by the conservatives, and it didn't wreck their economy.

Virtually every trained economist would agree with the statement that it is more economically efficient to collect tax revenue from products you are trying to discourage (alcohol, tobacco, emissions) than something you are trying to encourage (fresh food, books, work). The fact that the carbon tax debate was lost on economic grounds is the most exquisite demonstration of the power of econobabble.

(It's fun to note, by the way, that the party which introduced the GST also won the public debate about the carbon tax on the basis that it was 'a great big new tax on everything'. Well played!)

From the time that the carbon price was proposed at the 2007 election (by both John Howard and Kevin Rudd) to the time it was legislated in 2011, the Australian exchange rate surged from below US$0.70 in 2008 to US$1.10 in 2011 before plunging back to US$0.75 in 2015. The idea that a modest carbon price, rather than the impact of the mining boom, would 'destroy the competitiveness' of Australian exporters is simply absurd. But then again, so was the fact that Australia faced a 'budget emergency' back in 2013, when public debt was half the level that Scott Morrison assured the Australian public was sustainable in 2020.

Rising electricity prices played an important role in destroying popular support for the carbon price, but in fact these had almost nothing to do with the carbon price either. The carbon price did increase the average electricity bill by $172 per year – for which most houses received significant compensation – but the cost of 'distribution services' (commonly known as the 'poles and wires') pushed the average bill up by $580 between 2008 and 2014.[33] This, plus the costs of managing customers, advertising and paying profits to the owners of the electricity companies, was what was driving up electricity prices, but while the inefficiencies and profits associated with privatising the electricity sector drove up the prices, the carbon price took the blame. It was the scapegoat that distracted an entire nation from the truth. Again, well played!

Tony Abbott went to the 2013 election thundering about the 'budget emergency' and promising to 'axe the carbon tax'. What he didn't say was that while he was planning to scrap the carbon tax, he was also planning to keep the expensive tax cuts that had accompanied it. That is, he scrapped the new source of revenue and kept the expensive and inequitable new compensation. He was also happy for the companies that were paid billions of dollars in compensation for the carbon tax to hang on to the taxpayers' money, even though he was abolishing the thing they were being compensated for. Budget emergency? Not so much.

4. Because the sun doesn't always shine and the wind doesn't always blow, we can't rely on renewable energy.

> 'In Australia we need to get at least one or two of these [coal-fired power stations] built to ensure there's enough baseload power in the grid.'
> —Craig Kelly, former Liberal MP[34]

It is true that the sun doesn't always shine and the wind doesn't always blow, and it's also true that the wheat isn't always in harvest, the avocados aren't always in season and the so-called 'baseload' coal-fired power stations aren't always operating. Luckily for those who like to turn their lights on at night-time and have some avocado on toast with their latte, capitalism has developed lots of solutions to problems as predictable as night-time and calm days.

There are so many problems with the suggestion that without coal-fired power stations we can't have a reliable electricity system that it's hard to know where to start, but let's begin at the beginning and debunk the whole idea of 'baseload'. *Load* isn't really an economic term, but if we translate *baseload* into economics, it refers to the minimum amount of demand for electricity, which in Australia is the amount of electricity customers need overnight when most people and factories are asleep.

The Australian electricity system doesn't struggle to meet 'base demand'; it struggles at times to meet 'peak demand', which usually occurs on hot afternoons when the factories and offices are open and people start to turn air conditioners on in their homes. When these peaks in demand are greater than the capacity of all the different types of generation (coal, gas, solar, wind and hydro) we use to supply electricity, then blackouts occur. While coal-fired power stations can help to meet these periods of 'peak demand', it's important to realise that, at these times:

- the sun is very much still shining;

- the wind is usually blowing; and

- coal-fired power stations are the most likely to break down.

While the adjective 'reliable' is often inserted ahead of the term 'coal-fired power station', in reality the ageing fleet of coal-fired steam engines in Australia are quite unreliable. And because of their age and design, they are more likely to break down in the hot weather that usually accompanies peaks in our energy demand.[35]

It is true that if all the coal-fired power stations closed permanently tomorrow, we would have significant problems producing enough electricity to meet our current patterns of demand, but no one committed to reducing Australia's greenhouse gas emissions has seriously suggested the rapid shutdown that friends of the coal industry like to mock. The oldest coal-fired power station in the National Electricity Market (NEM) is at Liddell, New South Wales: it was commissioned in 1971. And the 'youngest' coal-fired power station in the NEM is at Kogan Creek, built in 2007. It is no surprise that fifty-year-old power stations will need to shut down soon, but it is perhaps surprising that in the last thirteen years, not one new coal-fired power station has been built.

As more and more wind and solar plants are built, and more and more batteries and hydro storage facilities are built, the less important the role of coal-fired power stations becomes. Despite the removal of the carbon price, private investors have continued to invest heavily in renewable energy for the simple reasons that it is cheaper to build new renewables than new coal-fired power stations, and that renewables have better long-term prospects.

When it comes to electricity, market forces and democratic forces are pushing in the same direction, but for reasons known only to themselves, many 'free marketeers' in Australia are determined to provide subsidies to build and maintain coal-fired power stations long after the accountants and investors have decided that is a bad use of investor capital.

CONCLUSION

The coal mining industry and coal-fired electricity generators are not big employers. They don't pay a lot of tax, but they do get a lot of subsidies.

There are lots of reasons to tackle climate change, only a handful of which are economic. As a society, we are usually willing to pay a small amount now to protect ourselves against future risk. We call it insurance. Few people, having spent a thousand dollars insuring their house against the unlikely risk of fire, feel they have 'wasted their money' when it doesn't burn down. Likewise, the outbreak of COVID-19 made clear that the overwhelming majority of the population, and politicians, were happy to put human safety ahead of the amount of economic activity.

Even if tackling climate change was somehow bad for the economy overall, as opposed to small parts of the economy that are already shedding jobs through automation, it would still be a good idea to avoid it. But in fact doing something about climate change is a bargain.

For reasons beyond the scope of this chapter, we have been trained to think about responding to climate change differently to how we respond to other structural changes. While people talk endlessly about the 'costs' of tackling climate change, who remembers hearing people talk about the costs of switching from video recorders to DVD players, or the costs of switching from film cameras to digital cameras? Let's be clear: those transitions resulted in hundreds of thousands of job losses and millions of stranded (household) assets. Businesses went broke (remember Kodak?) and 'mum and dad investors' lost money.

The economy is changing all the time. People lose and gain jobs all the time. Except when it comes to climate change, the business community and the so-called free-market economists typically applaud such change. Have you ever heard a business lobby argue that emails were destroying the postal industry, and that we should therefore oppose the use of email?

Carbon pricing is good policy, but there is no economic or political necessity to win the fight about carbon pricing first. Scrapping subsidies, opposing new coal mines on prime farmland, encouraging energy efficiency and subsidising renewable energy (at least until the coal subsidies are removed) provide easy, effective and politically popular ways to rapidly reduce greenhouse gas emissions.

While collecting more tax from pollution and less from other sources is a good long-term goal, it will be politically easier once the coal mining subsidies have been scrapped and the renewable energy industry has had more time to grow. Winning the political argument about climate change will never be easy, but as the cost of renewable energy and batteries continues to fall, and as the political and diplomatic pressure to act rises, it will become easier.

The big problem, however, is that unlike the pursuit of fairness, efficiency or environmental sustainability, the fight for climate policy has a deadline. While the rate at which digital cameras replaced film cameras was of little consequence, the rate at which the world reduces its consumption of fossil fuels will determine, for centuries to come, the average global temperature, the extent of sea-level rise and, in turn, the habitability of huge swathes of the planet.

The declining cost of, and increasing investment in, renewable energy in Australia is an indication of how close and cheap a clean energy future could be, but those who are concerned about solving the actual problem of climate change must never look away from the fact that if Australia succeeds in increasing exports of coal, oil and gas, then it will succeed in causing the climate change that our domestic renewable energy investment is designed to prevent.

While the vast majority of those who profit from the export of immense quantities of Australian fossil fuels are not Australian, they continue to have an enormous influence over Australian politics and policy. Defeating their political influence may be difficult, but winning an economic debate with an industry that employs so few people and pays so little tax should be easy. Once we strip away the econobabble.

What Really Causes Unemployment?

'If you have a go, you get a go.'
—**Prime Minister Scott Morrison**[1]

W hen it comes to unemployment, it is far easier to blame the victim than it is to solve the problem. And victim blaming remains the first instinct among many conservative politicians and 'economic commentators'. Scott Morrison's folksy assertion that if you have a go you get a go, like all successful slogans, works not because it tells us something new, but because it reminds of us of what we already think we know: that those who lack work probably lack the gumption to get it. Of course, Mr Morrison is far from the first politician to toot this dog whistle. John Howard talked of 'mutual obligation', Tony Abbott spoke of 'job snobs', and Joe Hockey, in his 2014 budget speech, announced his plan to make it harder for young unemployed people to access financial support, so that they would not 'embark on a life on welfare'. Under Hockey's 'plan' to tackle unemployment, those under thirty would have to wait up to six months before the government would give them any aid.[2]

Mr Hockey's plan to fix housing affordability was similarly patronising. Rather than fix the tax concessions for investment housing that have helped make Australian housing among the most expensive in the world, Mr Hockey opined that 'the starting point for a first home buyer is to get a good job that pays good money'.[3]

The idea that unemployment is caused by laziness and that good jobs go to those who work hard to find them is as old as it is baseless. Does anyone really think that the spike in unemployment in 1991, during the GFC – or, more recently, following the outbreak of COVID-19 – was caused by an outbreak of laziness? Does anyone really think that unemployment in regional communities – the communities most frequently represented by conservative members of the National Party – is so much higher than in our cities because country folk are lazier than the inner-city 'latte sippers'? And does anyone really believe that nurses and childcare workers earn, on average, so much less than financial planners because nurses and childcare workers don't work hard enough?

Unemployment is a uniquely complicated and multifaceted economic problem, made all the more difficult by the fact that the things that determine which individuals are more likely to be unemployed are unrelated to the things that determine why the number of unemployed people rises and falls in a matter of months. But despite this complexity, or perhaps because of it, simple solutions that simply do not work never lose popularity among those who have never experienced unemployment.

Like the failed attempts to get 'tough on drugs' and 'tough on crime', conservative politicians and business leaders seem to never tire of getting 'tough on the unemployed'. So much so that, during the deepest recession in modern history, the Morrison government cut the level of income support being paid to the unemployed on the basis of unsubstantiated claims that welfare payments were the cause of a 'worker shortage', despite ABS data showing there were more than a million people looking for additional work.[4]

It gets worse. As will be explained below, not only have successive governments blamed the unemployed for their unemployment, but they have done so while implementing policies designed to ensure that there is actually a minimum number of people who are unemployed, known as the 'natural rate of unemployment' or 'Non-Accelerating Inflation Rate of Unemployment' (NAIRU).[5] In short, no government in decades has pursued a policy of driving unemployment to zero; on the contrary, the federal government and the Reserve Bank of Australia always want around 600,000 people unemployed at any point in time. Their fear is that if unemployment accidentally falls below that level, inflation might rise.

The question for governments, then, is not 'How do we solve unemployment?' but 'How do we use the unemployed for our political advantage?' Unfortunately, blaming the victim is an easy way for governments to sidestep the need to solve the problem, while also signalling to the majority of voters who do have jobs that the government is on 'their' side. And siding with the majority is usually a good idea in a democracy. Econobabble plays a key role in concealing simple truths about unemployment, while supporting simplistic, and ineffectual, 'solutions'.

LABOUR MARKETS DON'T WORK THE WAY BUSINESS LEADERS SAY THEY DO

Most of what you have been told about how labour markets work is the kind of rubbish that would see you fail a first-year economics course. But that is hardly surprising, given that most of the people talking about wages and unemployment have no training in economics. While they may lack qualifications, they rarely lack confidence. And they certainly don't see a need to be consistent in their arguments. Consider the following:

- When the economy is growing rapidly, employer groups typically say it is a bad time to raise wages, as that would cause inflation. And when the economy is growing slowly, employer groups typically say it is also a bad time to raise wages, as that would cause more unemployment. So when would it be a good time to raise wages?

- We are always told that investors 'need certainty' in order to make long-term decisions, but that workers 'need to be flexible'. Why do we expect young people with no money to borrow tens of thousands of dollars to fund their degrees, with no certainty that their skills will be valuable in a decade's time, yet we accept that billionaires with diversified investment portfolios can't make a new investment unless governments promise them 'certainty'?

- Why do increases in wages supposedly cause inflation or harm our ability to export, but increases in profits are a sign that the economy is doing well? Why do we believe that record profits don't also drive up the cost of living?

- If the wealthiest and most productive economies in the world have high minimum wages, why would we as a nation pursue a lower minimum wage?

Economists call our workplaces the 'labour market', and the vast majority of trained economists would agree that it is one of the most complicated and hard-to-predict markets that exist. The reason it's so hard to analyse is that people are much less uniform than most other things economists study. Workers are different to each other, managers are different to each other, companies are different to each other, cultures are different to each other – and all of those differences keep changing. And to make matters worse, the demand for workers has more to do with the demand for the stuff they make than with the workers themselves. Firms don't employ people because they have skills or are cheap; they employ people because they need them to make stuff that people want to buy. Blacksmiths and bonnet makers didn't lose their jobs because they lost their skills or demanded higher wages; it was because people didn't want to buy the stuff they were skilled at making. If economists' simplistic model of 'perfect competition' struggles to explain the market for orange juice or coffee, what chance does it have in explaining how the labour market works?

But despite the widespread acceptance among trained economists that 'labour markets are different', conservative politicians and self-appointed 'business leaders' typically rely on arguments and analogies based on 'commonsense' ideas about what causes unemployment – and they're almost always wrong.

IF THERE WAS A SIMPLE SOLUTION TO UNEMPLOYMENT, WOULDN'T SOMEONE HAVE FOUND IT BY NOW?

Populist economic prescriptions are like fad diets. Don't eat meat. Don't eat fat. Don't eat carbs. Only eat meat. Fat is good but sugar is evil . . . The problem faced by real nutritionists is that there is no such thing as a 'super food' or 'slimming secret', and it's hard to sell books that don't promise something new.

People's metabolisms, like their prospects in the labour market, are all different. But no one ever lost weight while consuming more energy than they used up. And no government ever solved unemployment by training more workers than there were jobs available.

After hundreds of years in hundreds of countries, there is no agreed and foolproof solution to unemployment. While there is some agreement among economists about what does and doesn't work in the short term, there is very little agreement about what the 'best thing' to do about unemployment is. What we have instead are the equivalent of fad diets.

Consider the following 'fads' among the commentariat:

- In the 1980s, the Japanese economy was held up as the one we should emulate. Their rigid employment practices, the way they offered jobs for life to 'company men', and even their early-morning calisthenics were, we were told at the time, the reason for the Japanese economic miracle.

- In the 1990s, we were supposed to emulate the United States. Its 'flexible' labour market, low wages, lack of sick pay and holiday pay, and the way its service sector worked for tips, were, we were told, the reasons for the US economic miracle.

- The 'Asian Tiger' economies – of Hong Kong, Singapore, South Korea and Taiwan – briefly provided another model for us to emulate in the 1990s. They provided a combination of the US-style lack of basic protections for workers with much lower rates of tax than either the United States or Japan.

- The 'Celtic Tiger' economy of Ireland in the early 2000s briefly provided 'proof' that low taxes, especially for corporations, were the key to low unemployment. You don't hear much about copying Ireland since the global financial crisis of 2007–08.

In the first six months of 2020, the number of people employed in Australia fell by 4.9 per cent (632,200 people).[6] Of course, this collapse in employment had nothing to do with the laziness of job seekers, the skills of the previously employed, the design of Australia's industrial relations system or the level of wages. Employment collapsed for the simple reason that a large number of businesses had to close for health reasons, and an even larger number of Australians stopped spending money in places and on things that used to need workers.

While it's true that government decisions to close cinemas and shut our borders led to the direct loss of many jobs, it is not true that such decisions were unprecedented. The reduction of import tariffs in the 1990s led to tens of thousands of textile workers losing their jobs, many of them migrant women in regional areas. The privatisation of the Victorian electricity system in the mid-1990s led to more than 10,000 jobs being lost, most of them in the La Trobe Valley. And when Campbell Newman was elected Queensland premier in 2012, he sacked almost 13,000 public servants. Governments have a long history of making decisions that cost people jobs. What is new about COVID-19 is that there were so many victims of government policy that it was politically impossible to blame the victims. For a while at least.

Just as the Rudd government responded to the GFC by pumping money, and in turn demand for workers, into the economy, the Morrison government did the same thing, only on an even bigger scale. If low wages or more training was the best way to fix unemployment, then the Morrison government would not have committed more than $200 billion to new spending proposals.

The purpose of 'stimulus spending', whether it be for new public buildings or increased welfare spending, is to create demand for things that, in turn, create demand for people to produce those things. While conservative businesspeople and politicians like to talk about which people get jobs (expensively educated people like their children, with good references from people like themselves), in order to understand the reality of unemployment it is far more important to focus on how many jobs there are for the potential workers to compete for.

THE FALLACY OF COMPOSITION

One of the reasons labour market economics is so difficult to understand is the blurry line between why some individuals earn more than others (a micro-economic problem) and why average wages across the whole economy are rising faster or slower than average (a macro-economic problem). While micro-economics can help explain why some people are unemployed at the moment (they likely have lower levels of skill and experience than the employed), it can tell us nothing about why the ranks of the unemployed swelled by hundreds of thousands in the early 1990s. (Hint: it wasn't an outbreak of unskilfulness.)

Economics isn't unique when it comes to inconsistency between accepted theories. Physicists, for example, accept that the 'laws of physics', which help explain how cannonballs move through the air, have no predictive power when trying to explain how electrons move around. While physicists dream of developing a 'grand unified theory of everything', they accept that, for the time being, they need different models to explain big things and little things. They also accept that their model of big things and their model of little things are contradictory at times, and that, in some sense, both their models must be a bit wrong.

While most trained economists accept that our micro-economic model explaining why a particular individual is unemployed does nothing to explain the national unemployment rate, politicians and business leaders often ignore this simple truth. Their denial (or failure to understand) means that they can blame the unemployed for their joblessness, but it does nothing to help them solve the actual problem of mass unemployment.

Common sense says that what works for an individual should work for anyone else who tries it. Economists know that we can't make that assumption – it's simply incorrect. Indeed, it's an error made so commonly that we have a name for it: the 'fallacy of composition'.

Let's consider an example. If you steal biscuits or toilet paper from your workplace, you'll probably save yourself a bit of money on biscuits and toilet paper. But if you tell everyone at your work about your idea and everyone starts doing it, then your employers will probably install a vending machine for snacks instead, and one of those annoying toilet paper dispensers that only gives you one small piece of paper at a time. What works when one person does it doesn't work when everyone does it.

The same is true with car parking. Imagine your friends are complaining that they can never find a car park near the cafe you meet at, so you tell them where your 'secret parking spot' is. Do you think that the next time you and your friends arrange to go to the cafe, you will all find the same convenient secret park? What is true for the individual doesn't always hold true for the collective.

This is especially so for the labour market. If you were having trouble getting a job and I offered to call some friends and tell them what a great employee you were, I could probably get you a job – but I can't do that for lots of other people at the same time. You guessed it: what works for an individual doesn't work for a large group.

Remember Mr Hockey's comments about housing? He clearly didn't understand the fallacy of composition. He went on to say: 'If you've got a good job and it pays good money and you have security in relation to that job, then you can go to the bank and you can borrow money, and that's readily affordable.'[7] Mr Hockey was pilloried by his opponents for the insensitivity of his comment, but the fundamentally flawed logic of his advice went largely unremarked. At a competitive house auction, the market price will be determined by the bidders' willingness and ability to pay. Having a big deposit, a high income or generous parents will all help an individual 'win' at such an auction. But we can't all have better jobs than each other. That's Economics 101.

Likewise, we can't all be better trained than everyone else. Surges in unemployment are not evidence of a 'loss of skills', or of an 'outbreak of laziness'. They are evidence of a shortage of jobs relative to the number of job seekers. Training people to have better interview skills might change who gets a job, but it can't possibly affect how many people get a job.

Just as household analogies of budgets don't work very well for governments, individual stories about how to get a job aren't very useful for understanding how labour markets work. Everyone knows someone who is too lazy to apply for a job – and every conservative politician seems to know someone who applied for a hundred jobs before getting a job as a cleaner, and then went on to rise through the ranks of the company. Even if such stories are true, they are irrelevant when it comes to explaining why unemployment grew by 2.4 per cent in the months after COVID-19 hit.[8] Does anyone really think those 280,000 people suddenly became lazy?

BLAMING THE BLUDGER

Anyone suggesting that a simple fix for unemployment would be to fix all of the unemployed people is either lying to themselves about how much economics they understand, or lying to the public about how much economics they understand.

Politicians and businesspeople who think that their own personal story – or, worse, some story they heard about someone else – qualifies them to participate in a public debate about how to tackle unemployment should be laughed off the stage. What follows are three more of the most common but wrong-headed opinions about the employment market in Australia.

I. Unemployment is caused by bludgers who won't look for work or take the jobs on offer.

> 'We are getting a lot of anecdotal feedback from small businesses, even large businesses, where some of them are finding it hard to get people to come and take the shifts because they're on these higher levels of [JobSeeker] payment.'
>
> —**Prime Minister Scott Morrison**[9]

While this view is common among the conservative commentariat, it is a pretty harsh assessment of the country folk who typically vote for the National Party. Average unemployment rates are usually much higher in the bush than they are in the cities, so if the conservatives are right that unemployment is caused by the laziness or 'job-snobbishness' of the unemployed, then it would seem that growing up in the country has a terrible impact on work ethic. Of course, it's possible that there simply aren't enough jobs in rural areas for the people who live there.

2. The unemployed should move to find work.

> 'If people choose to live where there's no jobs, obviously it's very, very difficult to close the gap.'
>
> —**Tony Abbott in 2015, on the 'lifestyle choices'**
> **of Indigenous Australians**[10]

Have you ever noticed that the same conservatives who put so much emphasis on 'family values' are quick to encourage the unemployed to leave their families behind? And while they say Indigenous people should leave their ancestral lands behind in order to find work, they nevertheless insist that public money should be spent to keep farmers on land they have farmed 'for generations'.

The fact that most people need to live near their workplace is a major reason that 'labour markets' are harder to explain, and to fix, than markets for commodities such as fruit or computers. The 'social' and 'personal' reasons that people want or need to live in a particular place are significant. A large number of Australians have important roles caring for their elderly parents, and many others rely on support from their extended families. The idea that they should abandon such support and move, which in turn would create greater demand on publicly provided care services, is surely inconsistent with the idea of 'looking after your own' typically championed by conservatives.

3. The unemployed lack the skills employers require.

The strangest way to blame the unemployed is to finger them for lacking the experience that getting a job would give them. It's like blaming a starving person for not eating enough.

Imagine the following. There are two applicants for a job in a shop. One applicant has twelve months' experience and has completed a one-month course in retail management. The other has neither experience nor training. If all other things were equal (an economist's favourite assumption), who do you think would get the job?

But the politically convenient idea that unemployment in general is caused by a 'lack of skills' is economically flawed. The lack of trained mobile phone engineers didn't impede the rapid growth of the mobile phone industry, and the abundance of trained photograph development technicians did nothing to stop the collapse of the photographic film industry and the rise of digital cameras. Growing industries train the staff they need in order to keep growing.

Imagine that we wanted to 'fix' unemployment in a small country town of 1500 people, and we now 'know' that those with training and experience are more likely to get jobs than those without. In our small town there are thirty unemployed young people. Rather than let them 'waste their lives' on unemployment benefits, the government implements an 'earn or learn' policy and requires all of the town's unemployed people to do a course in retail management, and to do associated unpaid 'work experience'. Do you think that all thirty will be employed in a retail venture at the end of the course? In fact, do you think more or fewer people will be employed in the town's shops, since the young people are required to work in them for free? In what world does the number of trained retail workers determine the demand for products in a shop?

Employers don't employ people simply because they have skills, but because there is enough demand to justify employing people to provide the goods or services consumers want. Increasing the number of trained retail workers will no more increase the number of people employed in retail than increasing the number of car tyres produced would increase the number of cars sold.

Of course, well-targeted investment in education and training can be good for individuals, and for the whole economy. There is great evidence that suggests that such investment drives productivity growth and economic growth, and helps individuals to enjoy their work more. But it is a fallacy of composition to suggest that because we train people, jobs will be created for them. They won't, and to say otherwise is a cruel exercise in blaming the victim.

WAGES ARE TOO HIGH!

'Our merchants and masters complain much of the bad effects of high wages in raising the price and lessening the sale of goods. They say nothing concerning the bad effects of high profits. They are silent with regard to the pernicious effects of their own gains. They complain only of those of other people.'

—Adam Smith, *The Wealth of Nations*

Every conservative knows that high wages cause unemployment. One of the many problems with this belief is that rising wages and rapid job growth usually go hand-in-hand and, according to the Reserve Bank of Australia, low wage growth was one of the main causes of the slow economic growth Australia was experiencing before COVID-19 hit.[11]

As discussed above, the labour market is far more complicated than the markets for razor blades or orange juice. There is no clear evidence that increasing the minimum wage increases unemployment. Indeed, numerous US studies have shown that lowering the (state-determined) minimum wage often leads to increased unemployment.

One of the biggest problems in this 'debate' is that conservative commentators typically talk about 'common sense', and ask lots of 'businesspeople' for their 'expert advice'. In reality, many of the businesspeople who are asked this question have a large and obvious conflict of interest: they prefer to pay lower wages, so they can make larger profits. (And, for the conservatives, the only thing that works better than blaming unemployment on the greed of low-paid workers is blaming the unions that represent them.)

It takes effort and skill to run a business well, but it doesn't take an understanding of economics. The fact that businesspeople believe that reducing wages will lead to a reduction in unemployment is about as relevant as young people believing it's okay to text and drive because they have good reflexes. Self-belief and self-interest can be a heady brew, but listening to those who drink too heavily from it can have devastating consequences.

As we've seen, so-called 'common sense' about training unemployed workers easily leads people astray in debates about the labour market, and the same is true of 'common sense' about wages. While it is true that rising wages can lead to fewer jobs, it is also true that falling wages can lead to fewer jobs. Wages are not simply a 'cost to business' – they are the major source of income in Australia, and in turn play a major role in determining the demand for everything, from clothes and food to cars and holidays, and so for labour.

While cutting the wages of an individual working for a small business might lead to an extra shift being offered to someone else (or not), slowing the rate of wage growth across the economy might lead to whole retail chains shutting down.

This is probably the perfect time to start talking about macro-economics.

DO PEOPLE WHO GET PAY CUTS SPEND MORE OR LESS MONEY IN THE LOCAL SHOPS?

The next time you hear someone talking about the need to cut wages in order to boost employment, just ask them this: 'What will happen to consumer spending if we cut people's wages?'

The problem for the average conservative is that simple stories with lots of reference to 'common sense' are their stock in trade. And while common sense allegedly tells us that high wages cause unemployment, common sense also tells us that lower wages will reduce the amount of money that people will spend in shops. At this point, the econobabble usually goes up a notch as the 'expert' tries to shift the debate back to the personal failings of the unemployed.

The reason it is hard to answer the question is because it is a really hard question. Indeed, it's the kind of question that economists have been arguing about for centuries. The root of the problem is that wages are both a cost to business and the major source of income in the economy. It's easy enough to ignore the overall impact of lowering one person's wage at one small business. It is ridiculous, though, to ignore the overall impact of lowering the wages of millions of people.

But this is exactly what most conservatives do when they trot out their folksy anecdotes about the economy and how the greed of the poor is what causes unemployment. Remember, actual economics is a lot more complicated, subtle and contestable than the econobabble of shock-jocks and tabloid politicians.

Imagine a small town with 1500 people, three pubs and a high rate of unemployment. Let's suppose that one of the publicans uses some 'common sense' to talk the government into an experiment, in the hope of increasing employment. Having received the nod from the government, the town's 'top pub' is allowed to halve the wages of its bar staff. All of a sudden, the publican finds that her business is much more 'competitive', and she reduces her food and beer prices to attract more customers. It works, and before she knows it she is putting on more staff to cope with all her new customers.

After she reports her success to the government, the experiment is expanded and the other two pubs are allowed to slash their wages too. They quickly cut their prices to win their customers back. I'm sure you can see where this is heading. Things start to slow down at the top pub as their new customers drift back to the other two.

The fallacy of composition has reared its common sense–destroying head again. What was true for one pub doesn't hold true for all pubs. In fact, it's possible that the general cut in wages might lead to an overall reduction in beer and food sales, and ultimately a reduction in the number of staff employed.

Workers are customers as well, and this means that wages are not just a cost to business but also an injection of demand into the economy.

When a pub halves the wages of its staff, they probably won't spend as much on beer and grub themselves. Most businesspeople see their job (and their skill) as gaining an advantage over their competitors, and when they think about the opportunity of paying their workers less, they aren't thinking about the fact that their competitors will be able to do the same. Unfortunately, most businesspeople don't think as big as Henry Ford, who realised earlier than most that his workers were also his customers.

Evidence doesn't change the minds of most conservatives, but evidence and arguments can change the minds of the people they are talking to. Economists have spent hundreds of years arguing with each other about what causes unemployment, so it's unlikely that you will land a killer blow in any debate you have with a conservative. But you don't need to land a killer blow to win a debate; often you just need to make your opponent seem foolish and belligerent. Given the refusal of many conservatives to admit that training can't create jobs, and that economy-wide wage cuts can lead to job cuts, it's usually not hard to make them appear both.

And remember: the more econobabble they speak, the simpler you should make your follow-up question. The average observer can spot a bullshitter when they see one.

THE UGLY TRUTH

Okay, it's time to break the big news. Governments in Australia like to have at least half a million unemployed people at any point in time. It doesn't matter how skilled they are, or what the wage rate is. Successive governments in Australia have, for decades, sought to 'manage the economy' in such a way that the unemployment rate hovers around 5 per cent.

If unemployment falls 'too fast' and the unemployment rate gets 'too low', Treasury (the folk who advise governments on spending and taxing policy) and the Reserve Bank (the folk who set official interest rates) get nervous. They're afraid that the economy might become 'overheated' and cause inflation – and they fear inflation more than they dislike unemployment. So when the economy is growing fast and unemployment is falling, the Treasury and the RBA use the budget (fiscal policy) or interest rates (monetary policy) to put 'downward pressure on demand'. That's a polite way of saying 'create a bit more unemployment'.

You don't believe me? Here's the RBA describing how monetary policy works: 'Substantial rises in interest rates, designed to restrain inflationary booms, have been followed by contractions in demand and a reduction in inflation. Conversely, substantial interest rate reductions have been followed by periods of significantly faster growth.' When translated, this means that lifting interest rates slows the economy down, and lowering interest rates speeds it up – and rapidly growing economies create more jobs than slowly growing economies.

The problem for unemployed people is that the RBA usually starts to get 'nervous' about inflation whenever the unemployment rate gets below 5.5 per cent. Put another way, if there are fewer than 600,000 unemployed people in Australia, the RBA is likely to start trying to slow the economy down, in order to make sure inflation doesn't grow. This is good news for people who worry about inflation, and bad news for the 600,000 people who can't find jobs.

Why on earth would they do this, I hear you ask. It's a surprisingly simple question that is rarely put to treasurers and prime ministers. The best answer I can give you is that they fear that if they don't maintain a large pool of unemployed people, workers might be confident enough to demand higher wages; and employers, in turn, would increase the prices they charge for their products in order to cover the resulting higher wages. This is called a 'wage–price spiral', but with Australian firms facing stiff competition from imports, it's hard to see how they could simply pass on price rises in this way.

I wish I could give you a better answer, and I encourage you to ask others to explain it. After thirty years of asking, I'm yet to hear an answer I find persuasive.

Mentioning Marx isn't the best way to win an economic debate in Australia, but it's interesting to note that he, too, talked about employers' desire for a 'reserve army of labour' that would – you guessed it – keep 'downward pressure' on wages.[12]

SO IF WE CAN'T REDUCE UNEMPLOYMENT, WHAT CAN WE DO?

We could reduce unemployment if we wanted to. But successive governments have accepted the advice of Treasury and the RBA that to reduce unemployment below their estimate of its 'natural rate' (or Non-Accelerating Inflation Rate of Unemployment – NAIRU to its friends) of around 5 per cent will cause inflation. The good news is that in recent times the RBA has lowered its best guess about the NAIRU from 5.5 per cent to 4.5 per cent. The bad news is that still means that the RBA thinks we need to have at least 500,000 people unemployed to keep inflation low.

So, if we accept this premise (as prime ministers Howard, Rudd, Gillard, Abbott, Turnbull and Morrison have) and agree that we can't – or won't – reduce unemployment to anything like zero, what can we do? The main thing we can do is to increase the productivity of labour, and be nice to the people who are unemployed, as they are keeping inflation low for the rest of us.

Virtually all economists would agree that investment in general education and specific training are good ways to create more productive workers. And while productivity growth can be disruptive for those who, like the New South Wales miners, lose their jobs to machines, in the long run most people would prefer to live in a high-productivity (and high-wage) country such as Australia than in a low-productivity (and low-wage) country such as Bangladesh.

As discussed in Chapter 8, it is interesting to note that the conservative politicians who claim that they want to increase economic growth systematically refuse to invest more taxpayers' money in the thing that nearly all economists agree would boost economic growth in the long run: education for all.

But of course there is no need to accept the premise that we can't, or shouldn't, push unemployment down below 4.5 per cent, or any arbitrary number. Governments around the world embraced the ideas of John Maynard Keynes after World War II, and succeeded in driving unemployment down to near zero. After Keynesian stimulus was abandoned in the 1980s and '90s, we were told that the rise of unemployment was caused by greedy workers and 'inflexible' labour markets . . . but after decades of low wage growth and labour market deregulation we have not come close to getting unemployment back to where it was in the 1950s or '60s. While conservatives argue that this simply means we need even lower wage growth and even fewer labour market protections, even conservative institutions like the Reserve Bank of Australia and the Department of Treasury now freely admit that low wage growth is actually *causing* unemployment (as low-paid workers can't create much demand for work) rather than fixing it.

Since neoliberalism, with its obsessions with union busting and budget surpluses, came to dominate our approach to unemployment, new schools of thought – such as the post-Keynesians and modern monetary theorists – have found new reasons to agree with Keynes's old prescription that if there is high unemployment, then governments should spend more money to create more demand for work.

And since the outbreak of COVID, conservative governments around the world have 'spent money they don't have' to stimulate the economy. According to the Australian Treasury, the Morrison government's stimulus package has saved hundreds of thousands of jobs. And they are right.

There is no question that fiscal stimulus works to create jobs – the only question is whether people will still believe that after the COVID crisis recedes and only the economic crisis remains.

CONCLUSION

Econobabble is used to conceal the horrible truth about unemployment from the masses, and to blame unemployment on the victims of government policy. Ruthless, huh?

While most right-wing shock-jocks 'know' that higher wages cause higher inflation and higher unemployment, they probably have no idea that successive governments have deliberately sought to maintain half a million or so unemployed people in order to keep wages and inflation from growing 'too fast'. The unemployed play an essential role in our economy. They keep inflation down for the rest of us. But rather than thank them, we usually demean them. We blame unemployment not on the RBA's interest-rate policy but on the unemployed masses' lack of motivation and experience.

Conservatives tell fairytales about the handful of unemployed people who work their way to the top in order to hide the truth: that policy-makers target a minimum level of unemployment and use the budget and interest rates to ensure that we never have a 'shortage' of unemployed people. Of course, most conservative commentators have no idea what the RBA really means when it says the labour market risks becoming 'overheated'. The next time they tell you it's common sense that high wages cause unemployment, just ask them what they think the natural rate of unemployment is. If they don't know, you win. And if they do know, you win.

Unemployment isn't caused by 'job snobs'. It's caused by snobs who hate it when the economy starts creating 'too many jobs'.

Debt, Deficits and Budget Honesty

ach year, the US president spells out their accomplishments and their vision in the State of the Union address. Each year in Australia, the federal treasurer spells out the state of our finances and the government's latest savings measures in the Commonwealth budget speech. It says something about us that our politicians seem to be more worried about money than the Americans.

More econobabble is spoken about budget deficits and public-sector debt than about any other issue. Newspapers once reported on budgets with headlines like 'Beer and cigs up'. These days, there are sixteen-page budget supplements telling us about 'outyears' and 'forwards', and attempting to decode the kind of accounting trickery that now dominates the budget papers (and once led to the collapse of Enron).

Don't get me wrong – budgets do matter. How a government plans to collect taxes and spend money has a significant impact on individuals, communities, industries and the economy as a whole. But the way that the budget deficit or surplus has become a talisman that symbolises the superior morality of one side of parliament, rather than a fat report that shows how spending priorities have changed in the past twelve months, has done nothing to improve the quality of economic (or political) debate in Australia.

Like all econobabble, most of the debate around the budget is designed to conceal, not reveal. Australia is one of the wealthiest countries in the world, and we live at the wealthiest point in world history. If we want to continue to be one of the lowest-taxing countries in the world, then we won't be able to spend as much on schools, hospitals and transport as northern European countries do. And if we want to lower our tax collections even further, to emulate those of our South Pacific neighbours, then we will ultimately have to lower our health and education spending as well.

Budgets do not document the morality of a government, or its economic ability (whatever that might mean), but they do document a government's recent performance and its planned priorities. But over the past two decades the debate has shifted. We once asked, 'Do we want to spend more money on the services we value?' Now it is simply, 'Is the budget in surplus or deficit?'

The arrival of COVID-19 has done more to improve the quality of economic debate in Australia than all the Productivity Commission's reports combined. It wasn't just holidays that got cancelled when the coronavirus reached our shores. Having been elected in 2013 on a platform of repairing 'the debt and deficit disaster', the Coalition delivered six more years of budget deficits and growing debt, but COVID-19 forced them to abandon both the farce that Australia had ever had a 'budget emergency' and the idea that the Coalition would repay 'Labor's debt' anytime soon. When Tony Abbott won office in 2013, net Commonwealth debt was $160 billion[1], and by January 2020, just before COVID-19 hit, it had ballooned to $430 billion.[2] By December 2020, it had grown to $611 billion.[3] Which, to be clear, is of absolutely no economic concern. None. Nada. Zip. And on that the prime minister, the secretary of Treasury and the governor of the Reserve Bank all agree. It's as if everything the Coalition had said about budget deficits and public debt for seven years was complete crap . . .

WE NEED TO TALK ABOUT THE WORD *SURPLUS*

> *'All governments must unleash their balance sheets and invest in projects that create jobs now and continue to pay dividends into the future.'*
>
> **—The Business Council of Australia**[4]

Here, 'unleash their balance sheets' means 'borrow heavily'; after decades spent arguing that government borrowing was reckless and inefficient, presumably the BCA couldn't quite face admitting how wrong they had been, so they relied on a bit of econobabble instead. Words matter more than ideas in what passes for economic debate in Australia.

The fact that a budget deficit seems 'bad' and a budget surplus seems 'good' is a trick of language, not a truth of economics. *Surplus* is a positive word. We never say people put on weight because of a surplus of food; we say they overeat. And we don't say someone died from a surplus of heroin; we call it an overdose. Language also tells us that a *deficit* is something we should avoid – think of a learning deficit or an attention deficit disorder. But economics tells us no such thing about the relative merits of budget deficits and surpluses.

Simplistic analogies about managing household budgets make things even worse, and do nothing to help us understand the role of government budgets in managing the macro-economy. While the following pages will deal with the econobabble that dominates debates about our budget, we should first kill off the absurd notion that 'common sense' tells us that budget deficits are bad and surpluses are good.

In a speech entitled 'The Case for Change', Joe Hockey declared, 'To put it in the simplest terms, we are spending money we don't have.'[5] Putting complicated, multifaceted problems in their 'simplest terms' is often risky, but let's consider what would happen if anyone actually took the former Coalition treasurer's advice seriously:

- A responsible young person would never borrow money to fund their university degree (and a responsible government would never lend them that money as they have for the last thirty years).

- A responsible household would never borrow money to buy a house or a car.

- A responsible company would never borrow money to invest in a new factory.

- The Menzies government, which ran deficits for nine of its eighteen years in power, would have never borrowed money to build the Snowy Mountains Hydro-electric Scheme.

I know, I know, those 'deficits' are different because the people and companies that are 'spending like drunken sailors' and 'racking up debt' are actually making long-term investments. But did you know that the Commonwealth's budget deficit includes all of its capital spending on assets that will last for decades? And do you realise that spending Commonwealth money on education is specifically designed to increase Australia's gross domestic product in the future?

The idea that it is 'common sense' to never spend more than you earn makes absolutely no sense. It's not how people run their households, and it's not how businesspeople run their companies. For a government that can determine its own income (by varying taxes) and whose debts are written in a currency that it can issue, the notion is absolutely irrelevant.

COMPANIES DON'T ASPIRE TO RUN A BUDGET SURPLUS

'Households understand they must live within their means. Governments must do so too.'

—Tony Shepherd,
chair of Tony Abbott's National Commission of Audit, 2014,
and former president of the Business Council of Australia[6]

At the peak of the mining boom, a period in which world commodity prices were higher than they had been in a century, BHP and Rio Tinto were running budget deficits. They were spending more than they were earning. They were, according to Joe Hockey and Tony Shepherd's homespun wisdom, 'living beyond their means'.

BHP has been operating for 150 years and is still in debt. Its regular budget deficits mean that its debt has 'blown out' in recent years, but the company's board members and the shareholders aren't worried about BHP's 'profligacy'. Indeed, so unconcerned is the BHP board about the size of their budget deficit that it's never even mentioned in the company's annual report.

Read that again if you need to. Companies don't care about their 'budget deficit' or 'budget surplus'. They don't even talk about them. They do talk about their profits a lot, but a *profit* and a *surplus* are entirely unrelated concepts. Econobabblers suggest they are the same, but they are not calculated in the same way and they do not mean the same thing.

Just as our brains tell us that deficits are bad and surpluses are good, years of econobabble have trained most people to think of a budget surplus as the public-sector equivalent of a profit, and a budget deficit as a loss. But again, we must understand that a *deficit* and a *loss* are entirely different things. For centuries, priests told us that the earth was the centre of the universe – but just saying it for a long time doesn't make it true.

WHY *RUNNING A SURPLUS* IS NOTHING LIKE *MAKING A PROFIT*, AND WHY PEOPLE WHO SAY IT IS ARE EITHER IGNORANT OR LYING

A budget surplus exists when you receive more money in a given period than you expend in that period. When a surplus is distributed to its owners – such as when Kevin Rudd's government posted everyone a cheque for $900 during the GFC – that is treated as money going out, and so reduces the size of the surplus. Now, hold that thought.

A profit means that more money was received in a given period than was spent to produce it. Unlike a surplus, a profit does not treat the full cost of buying long-lived assets (such as a house, a factory or a piece of machinery) as an expense to be deducted from the revenue received in that period. Also unlike a surplus, if a company paid a dividend of $900 to each of its shareholders, that 'return of funds to owners' would not be treated as an expense, and so would not be deducted from the calculated profit of the firm.

The 'reckless governments' that are 'spending irresponsibly' and creating a 'burden' for future generations are actually spending an enormous amount of money today that will deliver benefits for future generations. Indeed, if you took all of the capital spending out of the budgets and treated it separately (as governments used to do), then you would see that recurrent spending (which also includes spending on things that create future benefits, such as education) is usually less than recurrent revenue.

All of that 'unaffordable' welfare spending is, it seems, entirely affordable – even taking into consideration our desire to remain as one of the lowest-taxing nations in the developed world, and our agreement for high-income retirees not to pay a cent in tax on their multimillion-dollar retirement incomes, and our willingness to let multinational companies such as Apple and Google pay virtually no tax here.

Imagine what we could 'afford' to do if we chose to collect the OECD average rate of tax each year. In 2018–19 that would have meant more than $100 billion in additional revenue that we could spend on extra services if we wanted to. That could fund quite a bit of investment in schools, roads and hospitals, with plenty left over to balance the budget, if that's what we wanted to do. But we don't – or, more precisely, our elected representatives don't.

CONSERVATIVES LOVE BUDGET DEFICITS

In 2014, the Coalition government said we were 'living beyond our means' and faced a 'budget emergency', which, if not addressed, would lead us 'into the eye of an economic storm'.[7] Sound scary? Relax. Joe Hockey did.

In 2015, then treasurer Hockey announced that even though the deficit had grown, the storm had passed. Indeed, during his 2015 budget speech he was decidedly chipper. In twelve months he shifted from preaching doom and gloom to urging everyone to look on the bright side of life. He used his budget speech to tell Australians to 'have a go'.

In his 2019 budget speech, treasurer Josh Frydenberg prematurely, and optimistically, announced that the budget was 'back in surplus'. What he meant to say was that his Department of Treasury had forecast that the budget might be back in surplus sometime soon. It wasn't. And it won't be anytime soon. Not only did the lockdowns that accompanied COVID-19 reduce the size of the economy and, in turn, the amount of tax collected, but the Morrison government announced enormous new spending measures like JobKeeper and the JobSeeker supplement. But despite the biggest budget deficit since World War II, and despite seven years of rhetoric about the need to deliver a budget surplus and repay public debt, the Morrison government introduced expensive, and permanent, tax cuts. If conservatives really are worried about budget deficits, then why do they keep causing them with expensive tax cuts?

American conservatives have a name for their strategy of causing budget deficits in order to justify future cuts to services: they call it 'starving the beast'. I call it the 'right-wing ratchet', and it works like this.

When the economy is booming, you cut taxes for the wealthy. You tell people it will be 'good for the economy', and that 'the markets will respond well'. A few years later, when the economy and tax revenue begin to falter, you say you have 'no choice' but to cut spending on the poor. Introduce co-payments, tighten welfare eligibility criteria and, if you're feeling particularly brave, cut taxes for the wealthy again. Tell the punters that the tax cuts will 'give investors confidence', and that 'the markets will respond well'. Better yet, rebadge the tax cuts for high-income earners as 'investment incentives'. Everyone loves incentives, and investment. They are good words.

When the economy is going well, deliver for the rich, and when the economy is going badly, you guessed it, cut spending on the poor. Reagan did it, Howard did it, Trump did it and Morrison is doing it. Don't ever tell yourself that the conservatives don't have a plan for the long run. They do, and it's a ripper for their biggest supporters.

It's hard to believe that such a simple strategy could work so well. But then again, it's hard to believe that priests of some religions managed to make entire populations feel guilty for having sex, or to insist that only men could be leaders. Just as speaking in Latin can make the ridiculous seem plausible, so can talking in econobabble. Especially when the journalists nod along instead of asking politicians what on earth they are talking about.

WHERE DID THE BUDGET EMERGENCY GO?

Magicians know that the easiest things to make disappear are things that were never there. The only people who reported seeing a budget emergency were the same ones who later assured us it had moved on. So what happened?

Tony Abbott was elected on the 'magic pudding' platform of cutting taxes, not cutting spending and rapidly reducing the budget deficit. It was never going to happen. Ahead of the 2103 election, when pushed to promise not to break his impossible commitments, Mr Abbott did so:

> Reporter: The condition of the budget will not be an excuse for breaking promises?

Tony Abbott: Um, exactly right. We will make, we will keep the commitments that we make.[8]

When challenged on their decision in 2014 to introduce new taxes and cut spending which they had promised not to cut, Joe Hockey, entirely predictably, stated: 'Well, okay, if we are arguing what people said, gee whiz, I wish the other mob had told us how bad the budget was.'[9]

The political strategy was simple:

- Step 1: Cut a range of taxes (such as the carbon tax and the mining tax).

- Step 2: Hold a Commission of Audit to 'discover' that the budget was in 'worse shape' than expected.

- Step 3: Introduce cuts to welfare and government services on the basis that to do otherwise would be 'fiscally irresponsible'.

The right-wing ratchet was designed to work over decades, but Abbott and Hockey tried to jump from tax cuts to big business to co-payments and welfare cuts in less than six months. They were never going to get away with it.

In addition to their unseemly haste, the problem for the Abbott government was that while a majority of the Senate voted to cut taxes, a majority of senators could not be found to support cuts to the aged pension or a wide range of other proposed cuts. That's when things got interesting.

After spending the months following the 2014 budget thundering about the impending budget crisis and the need for the Senate to bow to the government's will, despite its lack of an electoral mandate, Joe Hockey finally began to realise that the Senate might not be bluffing. And, as he began to put together his second budget, he realised that in order to slay the 'budget emergency' he had told people existed, he might have to collect more tax revenue.

The then treasurer started to talk about the need to rein in the tax concessions for superannuation, which cost the budget tens of billions of dollars each year and flow almost entirely to the top half of earners. He talked of the need to collect more tax from multinational companies. And he even hinted at a new tax on the banks. Documents obtained under freedom of information legislation make clear that the Treasury was working on new revenue measures to fill the government's 'budget black hole'.

And then Peter Costello hit the roof. In a flurry of stinging articles, the former treasurer, and the architect of the twenty-year plan to 'starve the beast' in Australia, called on the Abbott government to cut taxes to fix the 'budget emergency'. Yep, you read that right. Peter Costello argued that 'the government needs to restart the conversation about getting taxes down, not up'.[10]

PROFLIGATE PETE AND THE TAX CUTS THAT BROKE THE BUDGET

Poor Joe Hockey. It wasn't his fault that Chinese demand for resources collapsed on his watch. Similarly, it wasn't his fault that the tax cuts and loopholes introduced by Peter Costello at the beginning of the mining boom have undermined the ability of our tax system to collect much revenue even when the economy is growing.

Joe Hockey's problem was the flipside of Costello's claim to be a 'great economic manager'. Put simply, the world economy has a much more significant impact on the 'performance' of Australian treasurers than Australian treasurers have on the world economy. But politics, like astrology, always needs to conflate causation with correlation. If it happened *after* I did something, it must have happened *because* of what I did.

It wasn't Gough Whitlam who caused the 1973 OPEC oil crisis and the collapse of the world economy. It wasn't Costello's budget surpluses that caused China to double its demand for our natural resources in the mid 2000s. And, despite what the Coalition argues, the meltdown of the global financial system and subsequent world recession in the late 2000s wasn't caused by Wayne Swan.

In reality, most of the movement in monthly economic indicators is driven by events beyond our borders, or by policy decisions made years earlier. Indeed, the budget emergency that once worried Joe Hockey had its genesis in the permanent tax cuts that Peter Costello introduced in response to a temporary spike in tax revenue at the beginning of the mining boom.

According to economists at the International Monetary Fund, Peter Costello was Australia's most profligate treasurer of the past fifty years.[11] That is, according to the global doyens of fiscal responsibility, the man described by John Howard as Australia's greatest treasurer spent like a drunken sailor when the economy was booming. In doing so, he poured fuel on the mining boom's fire, pushed up interest rates for those with mortgages, and helped cause the budget deficits that Joe Hockey was so worried about in 2014.

If Peter Costello was such a 'good economic manager', then how come in his time as treasurer we were never rich enough to give aged pensioners a pay rise, or to cut the price of medicine for sick people, or to invest heavily in renewable energy? Peter Costello gave away a fortune in tax cuts to the wealthy, and he simultaneously 'saved' billions of dollars by making the lives of the sick and the elderly harder than they needed to be. By his own criteria, that made him a 'great economic manager'. But by the IMF's definition it made him profligate and short-term. I prefer the adjectives the director of the Liberal Party used to describe the perception of Costello's government after the 2001 election: mean and tricky.[12]

BUT COSTELLO DELIVERED ELEVEN SURPLUSES IN A ROW!

Most people remember that Peter Costello delivered a string of budget surpluses. But what most people don't remember is that it was Peter Costello who convinced them that the definition of 'good economic management' was running a budget surplus. Even fewer people will admit that they have little idea what a budget surplus really means. Econobabble is used to conceal, not reveal.

Anyone who has ever bought a house or a new car has run a 'budget deficit'. If you earn $100,000 per year and buy a $700,000 house, you will rack up a big deficit that year and, inevitably, a big debt. Is that reckless or irresponsible? Most people, and most financial planners, don't think so. Nor do most companies.

Tony Shepherd, the man who ran the Abbott government's Commission of Audit, and who told the nation it had to live within its means, knows the value of debt better than most. During his time as chairman of Transfield, its debt ballooned from $282 million to $1.606 billion.[13]

Peter Costello played a simple trick on the Australian people during the Howard years. While economists see budget deficits and budget surpluses as tools to help manage the economy, 'Profligate Pete' redefined the budget outcome as the ultimate objective of economic management. Put simply, he convinced us that surpluses were good and deficits were bad. So if he delivered a surplus, he must have done a good job. Right? Wrong.

Costello squandered a mining boom and convinced millions that he'd saved the country. His enormous and inequitable tax cuts were so poorly timed that they forced the Reserve Bank to push up interest rates, which in turn cost middle-income earners with mortgages a fortune.

The existence of a budget surplus or deficit is not evidence of good or bad economic management. What does matter, however, is that the size of the surplus or deficit is appropriate for the economic conditions of the time, and that the composition of government spending sets the country up for the future. Costello used econobabble to conceal the complexity of the problems he faced, and to justify his simplistic goal to cut taxes for his friends and cut public spending on his foes.

In economic management, as in politics, timing is everything. While government budgets are an annual affair, economies have much longer cycles than the time taken for the earth to get around the sun. All sorts of unexpected shocks – some good, some bad – affect our economy, and whether they cancel each other out or reinforce each other in an arbitrary twelve-month period has far more to do with luck than with economic management. A booming China was great for some parts of the Australian economy in the middle of the 2000s, and the GFC was terrible for other parts of the economy towards the end of that same decade. More recently, COVID-19 has decimated airlines and travel agents and delivered huge windfalls for many online retailers. And of course China's trade boom continues to deliver enormous profits to those with the right to export Australia's iron ore, but the arbitrary restrictions imposed on Australian exports to China have simultaneously delivered an enormous bust for those accustomed to selling lobsters, barley, timber and a range of other commodities to China's 1.4 billion consumers. The impact of the 'cold trade war' between Australia and China, and the uselessness of our supposed 'free trade agreement', are discussed in the next chapter.

The ups and downs of the Australian economy are known as the business cycle. While academic economists argue about definitions and measurement, the economy tends to slow down down every seven or eight years. By the middle of the 2000s, Australia was about 'due' for a recession.[14] But we got lucky. Instead of a slowdown, we got the biggest resources boom we had seen in a century. The prices for our biggest exports rose rapidly, as did corporate profits and corporate tax receipts. The impacts were obviously good for the budget's bottom line.

But rather than stockpile this temporary increase in revenue, Costello introduced permanent tax cuts. He cut by half the tax payable on income from capital gains. He trebled the threshold for the top tax bracket. He made income from superannuation entirely tax-free, even for those who earned millions per year. He also handed out tens of billions of dollars' worth of benefits to middle- and high-income earners, while arguing that the government couldn't afford to increase unemployment benefits, disability benefits or the aged pension.

The windfall revenue from the mining boom was so great that, despite Costello's largesse, the budget was still in surplus. With repetition, and with vocal support from a cheer squad of 'business leaders', he convinced people that simply delivering a surplus proved that he was doing a great job.

But the idea that a budget surplus is proof of good policy has no basis in economics. Imagine an ice-cream shop in a small beach resort. In the summer months it does a roaring trade; in the winter months it's a nice quiet place for the staff to read. Now imagine that you are the owner of the shop. In the middle of a long and hot summer, you see an ad for the car of your dreams. With ice-cream sales at record highs, you would still be in surplus even after the enormous monthly repayments. Would you buy the car on that basis?

According to the pinko lefties at the IMF, Peter Costello hosed our mining boom up against a wall. Indeed, according to the Reserve Bank of Australia, Costello's tax cuts and middle-class welfare pumped so much money back into the booming economy of the late 2000s that he forced the RBA to increase interest rates to 'take the heat' out of the economy.[15] (That's another nasty economic phrase that not enough people understand. When the RBA says it is increasing interest rates to 'take the heat' out of the economy, what it really means is 'increase everybody's mortgage repayments to lower their disposable income in the hope that they spend less money in the shops and cause a bit of unemployment'.)

Tens of billions of dollars' worth of tax cuts and new benefits were pumped back into an economy that was already booming. Virtually all economists agree that such fiscal stimulus when the economy is already booming is the exact opposite of responsible economic management, whether you are running a budget surplus or not. Theory and history say such stimulus would push up inflation and interest rates. Which is exactly what happened. Costello could have instead poured the money into the infrastructure a rapidly growing population would need. He could have invested in renewable energy, public housing or any other big investments that would have boosted both short-term employment and long-term productivity growth while delivering benefits to the community for decades to come. But he gave it to his friends as inflationary tax cuts instead and declared himself a great economic manager.

Costello must have known his tax cuts and middle-class spending splurge were economically irresponsible. Treasury told him, the RBA told him, the IMF told him. But he wasn't doing economic policy; he was doing politics. He owned the ice-cream shop during a hot summer, gave away free ice-cream to all his friends and still delivered a budget surplus. The books looked okay during his tenure, but all the freebies meant that the coming winter would be long and impoverished.

But Costello wasn't stupid. He wasn't trying to 'manage the economy' – he was trying to reshape it in a way that was more pleasing to his eye. He wanted to shrink the public sector and let the market provide more of our health, education and welfare services. But to achieve his vision, Costello had to cause budget deficits in the future, deficits big enough to scare the public into accepting big cuts to the services and safety nets that Australians are quite proud of. While it was easy for Costello to sell the tax cuts during the boom, the big cuts in spending in the future would be a tougher sell. That task fell to Joe Hockey, and he failed at the first hurdle.

Since winning office on the back of the imaginary 'debt and deficit disaster', the Abbott, Turnbull and now Morrison governments have been unable to implement the spending cuts that Peter Costello's tax cuts were based on. The result, pre-COVID, was six Coalition budget deficits in a row, and post-COVID will be budget deficits for the foreseeable future. While here budget deficits are of little economic consequence, they will be of enormous political consequence for years to come.

When the COVID-19 crisis passes, the Coalition will, inevitably, use the record levels of debt they have delivered to demand wide-ranging cuts to spending on people they don't like – probably younger people on welfare, the higher education sector, the ABC and the arts sector generally. While these cuts will all be framed, yet again, in the econobabble of 'budget emergency', the proof that no such energy exists is that, in the middle of the crisis, Scott Morrison and Josh Frydenberg did exactly what Peter Costello did and introduced enormously expensive income tax cuts. If they were at all worried about the size of the post-crisis deficit, they would have delayed or abandoned those income tax cuts, but instead they brought them forward. The right-wing ratchet never stops putting downward pressure on the size of the state – and the size of our ambitions for that state.

SO IS DEBT GOOD OR BAD?

Like a budget deficit, debt is neither good nor bad. It's just debt. What can be thought of as good or bad are the decisions we make about what it is worth borrowing money to fund, and what things we might miss out on because of our reluctance to borrow.

Debt simply allows us to bring expenditure forward in time. If we bring forward good ideas, we can increase our future income. If we bring forward bad ideas, then when we repay the money with interest we will have less to spend in the future. Again, it is not debt that is good or bad – what matters is the assets we are investing in or missing out on.

Consider the following:

- A young person could work until they have saved up enough money to pay up front for their uni degree and then graduate with no debt. Or they could borrow the cost of their degree and go to uni ten years earlier.

- A young family could rent until they have saved up the full price of a house and buy a home with no debt. Or they could save up a deposit, take out a mortgage and buy a home decades earlier.

- A small business owner could save up all of the funds needed to open a new store in a new location. Or they could borrow money against the existing business, and set up the new shop years earlier.

What all three of the above scenarios have in common is that debt allows the borrower to bring a good idea forward. The cost of bringing a good idea forward is the interest we pay on the borrowed funds. And the benefits of bringing a good idea forward in the above examples are:

- swifter access to a high-paid job;

- the ability to avoid rent and to accumulate capital gain on a house; and

- earlier access to the flow of profit that will come from opening a new shop.

Economics 101 does not teach us that 'debt is bad'. Rather, it suggests that a rational decision-maker should always pursue options in which the benefits exceed the costs.

But let's think about the alternative. If we agree with the idea that debt is simply bad, then the determination to avoid debt would lead us to avoid good investments whose returns would far exceed the cost of interest. The desire to be 'debt-free' would lead us to accumulate fewer of the assets we need for future prosperity. Such an approach has become synonymous with 'good politics', but it is entirely unrelated to notions of 'good economic decision-making' – except in the minds of those who, like Peter Costello, believe that all public spending is a bad idea.

The pursuit of 'deficit reduction' as an end in itself would lead governments to:

- avoid all investment in effective preventative health measures;

- cut all spending on schools and higher education;

- endure the costs of climate change rather than invest in things that might prevent them; and

- sell all public assets – even those that pay dividends of 10 per cent.

Households that want simply to 'repay debt' can do so – by selling their homes. Indeed, by Joe Hockey's logic, parents with a mortgage who send their kids to expensive private schools should stop doing so and direct all their funds towards repaying their home loan. But these parents presumably believe that the benefits of investing in their children's education are worth much more than the interest they pay on their mortgage. It's a pity more politicians don't think like that.

Just as conservatives define 'good economic management' as running a budget surplus, they claim that 'reducing debt' should be a goal of government policy. Using hackneyed and fundamentally flawed household analogies about 'living within your means', Peter Costello, Tony Abbott and Joe Hockey made their failure to invest in Australia's future look like evidence of their concern for future generations. Ever the pragmatist, Scott Morrison has shifted the language he uses about debt to distinguish between 'good debt' and 'bad debt'. While it is true that borrowing to go on a holiday will deliver fewer tangible lasting benefits than borrowing to buy a new home, it's also true that Morrison's use of 'good debt' and 'bad debt' broadly translates to 'the Coalition's debt' and 'Labor's debt'.

Borrowing money to boost spending can create jobs in the short term and deliver lasting benefits for decades to come. During the Great Depression, some of the stimulus was spent building beautiful Art Deco ocean baths that still deliver joy nearly a century later. There is nothing in economic theory that says borrowing is bad, and there is nothing in economic theory to clearly distinguish between good debt and bad debt. Such distinctions are ultimately democratic ones about priorities, not economic ones. But what better way to stifle debate about whether we should spend more money on tax cuts or renewable energy than to insist that such a debate is a purely economic one, to be conducted in the language of econobabble?

GOVERNMENTS SHOULD BORROW MORE THAN HOUSEHOLDS, NOT LESS

The average household in Australia has total debts of around $213,000.[16] As a proportion of household income, on average Australian households carry 150 per cent debt. The net debt that the government holds on our behalf, however, accounts for only 17 per cent of our national income. That's down from 41 per cent when Menzies left office. The OECD average, meanwhile, is 51 per cent.[17]

It makes sense for households to aim to repay most of their debts before they retire. For most Australians, retirement means that the most expensive stages of life (buying a house and raising kids) have passed. And most retirees' income falls when they leave the workforce (only the very rich and the unemployed get a pay rise when they turn sixty-five). But when will Australia retire?

Despite decades of our being told otherwise, nation-states are not like households in any significant sense.

Unless a government plans for Australia to retire at some point soon, then it makes no economic sense to repay all the nation's debts by some arbitrary deadline. Of course debt means that interest payments must be made, but as with a HECS debt or a mortgage, what is relevant is whether the benefits the nation has gained exceed those costs.

Far from retiring, Australia is growing very rapidly. Some 4 million people moved to Australia last decade, and so the need for new investment in schools, roads, hospitals, trains, police stations and sewers is enormous. Indeed, the budgetary cost of population growth far exceeds the cost of population ageing.[18]

Schools, roads and sewers last for decades. Indeed, as the Romans showed, if built well, roads will deliver benefits to future taxpayers for centuries. So why should this generation of taxpayers bear the whole cost – by paying cash up front – for infrastructure that will deliver benefits to many generations to come? Why should the cost of building new schools and hospitals come out of existing funding for teachers and nurses?

That's what 'starving the beast' is all about. To Peter Costello, Joe Hockey and Tony Shepherd, our schools, hospitals, aged-care homes and public transport system are 'the beast'. While other countries are investing heavily in education, renewable energy and public transport, Australia is cutting back. Someone is going in the wrong direction.

CONCLUSION

As we've seen, cutting taxes when the economy is booming is not 'good economic management' – it's really irresponsible. And, according to the RBA, when Treasury and Scott Morrison delivered the biggest budget deficit in modern history, it was the sensible and responsible thing to do after COVID-19 had smashed into the Australian economy.

Running a surplus has never been 'proof' of good economic management, but if you can convince the public it is, then you will have a much easier time convincing them that governments have 'no choice' but to cut spending on welfare, health and education. Of course, living in one of the richest countries in the world means we have an enormous range of choices. The purpose of econobabble about the budget is, however, to conceal those choices from the vast majority of the public so that they can be quietly made by a minority of the public.

But COVID-19 didn't just leave Josh Frydenberg's forecast budget surplus in tatters, it ripped up the conservatives' rhetorical and political playbook. From the opposition benches in 2009, the Liberal–National Coalition raged against the 'waste' and 'recklessness' of the Rudd government's GFC stimulus package, but when in government they not only took the same advice to spend, spend, spend, but they took a much bigger dose.

It is inevitable that the economy will begin to grow after the COVID-19 heath restrictions are removed. It is also inevitable that both the level of debt and the number of unemployed people will remain high for years to come. While there is no economic necessity to repay public debt by any arbitrary deadline, or indeed at all, the political case for doing so will be driven by conservatives who have a strong personal desire to spend less money on groups they don't like.

As Joe Hockey and Tony Abbott discovered, it is much easier to deliver big tax cuts in a boom than it is to deliver big spending cuts in a bust, especially after you have just rushed through big income tax cuts for high-income earners. But if the Coalition doesn't commit to 'budget repair' and 'paying down the debt to protect future generations', then how will they constrain the public's demands for more and better-quality public services?

Democracy, not economic theory, will determine the size and shape of government spending in the years that follow the COVID-19 crisis – but economics, not econobabble, will determine the impact of the decisions elected representatives make about how much money to spend, and on what. Whether or not we spend billions of dollars on renewable energy and public housing or gas pipelines and tax cuts will have a significant impact on the shape of our economy for decades to come. Any additional spending during a period of high unemployment will 'create jobs', but not all forms of public spending will deliver lasting benefits.

The Truth about the Free Market

'I don't need to tell you how critical that is for private-sector growth, and certainly the recovery phase that we all want to see come on as quickly as possible from COVID. It will form the basis of long-term viability, if we have good quality regulatory bodies like yourselves.'
—**International development minister Alex Hawke telling Pacific Island countries how important regulation is**[1]

Big businesses are built on red tape and regulation. They love it. The big banks, the big miners and the big software companies wouldn't be big without it. Indeed, big business loves regulation so much that their balance sheets often record the value of it as an 'asset'. Regulation helps to keep competitors out and prices up. Regulation limits the claims for damages that employees and customers can make against companies, and, of course, regulation forces us to buy products that many of us don't want. Without regulation, the legal, accounting and lobbying businesses wouldn't exist.

But econobabble about the 'burden of red tape' and 'the

need for regulatory certainty' allows business groups, and their apologists in parliament and the media, to walk both sides of a pretty wide street. When businesses oppose a regulation because it will cost them money, they use terms like *red tape*, *nanny state* and *individual choice*. They almost inevitably talk about the *burden* and the *cost* of regulation, and (as discussed in Chapter Seven) often produce reports with absurdly precise estimates of the alleged 'cost to the economy' of the laws they don't like.

But when businesses like a regulation because it will make them money, the econobabble takes on quite a different accent. In that case, strong economies are based on 'stable regulation' or, intriguingly, 'responsive regulation'. *Responsive* is just econobabble for 'governments should do what we tell them to'.

Put simply, the costs and benefits of regulation are in the eye of the beholder. And the role of econobabble is to make some beholders seem more credible than others. Apparently, when 'the markets' (translation: people who own a lot of shares) say we need regulation, governments should listen, but when the voters demand it, governments should 'resist populism'.

In the debate about the size and shape of regulation in Australia, the strategy of business groups is pretty simple: they privately love the regulations they love, and they publicly hate the regulations they hate. It's much easier for business groups to pretend to hate all regulation, and to pretend that all regulation will 'cost jobs' and 'reduce confidence', than it is to win a public debate about which kinds of regulation are in the national interest, and which are simply in the interests of the businesses demanding them.

Don't believe me? Consider this. The business community is forever calling for 'labour market deregulation', and in 2006 the Howard government delivered them the WorkChoices legislation – which amounted to 1000 pages of regulation. It took a lot of new regulation to deregulate the labour market, but the business community was happy nonetheless. Business groups don't hate all regulation – they just hate the regulations they hate.

BUSINESSES LOVE THE REGULATIONS THAT FORCE US TO BUY THEIR PRODUCTS

> 'Despite our belief that less regulation is better, the reason Australia has a stable payments system is due to regulation the RBA has enacted, for both Visa and MasterCard, along with abolishing the "no surcharge" rule with respect to all schemes.'
>
> **—Australian Retailers Association**[2]

Australians are forced by government regulation to spend 9.5 per cent of their income buying superannuation. In fact, the average Australian household spends more money each year on superannuation *fees* than it does on electricity.[3]

Of course, the premise underlying compulsory superannuation is that individuals can't be trusted to make their own decisions – but you don't hear the finance industry complaining about the way that regulation is 'stifling freedom'.

The superannuation industry, which prides itself on the bewildering array of 'choice' it offers consumers, will never support the removal of the laws that force all working Australians to buy their products. It's one thing to make customers choose between tens of thousands of superannuation products, but letting people decide for themselves how much superannuation they want to contribute when they are saving up to buy a house – that's going way too far.

It's a similar story with private health insurance, which Australians who earn above average incomes are effectively forced to buy. In this case, of course, you can 'choose' to not buy private health insurance, but if you do make that choice you have to pay an extra 1 per cent in income tax for those singles on $90,000 per annum (sliding up to 1.5 per cent for higher income earners) – an amount which is more than the cost of a cheap private health insurance policy.[4] Again, it is rare to hear the private health insurers complain about regulation and the need to 'empower' individuals to make their own choices.

Licensed electricians support regulations that prevent amateurs from wiring their own houses; pharmacists love regulations that prevent new pharmacies being built within 1.5 kilometres of their shops; coal-seam gas companies love the regulations that permit them to drill on farmers' land even if the farmers don't want to allow it.

REGULATION IS A GREAT IDEA, AND ECONOMIES COULDN'T WORK WITHOUT IT

None of this is to say that regulation is a bad idea – it's not. Banning asbestos was a good idea. Banning cigarette advertising was a good idea. Taking lead out of petrol was a great idea. And I am yet to meet a libertarian who thinks that anyone who wants to call themselves a surgeon should be free to do so.

The former senator David Leyonhjelm, a self-described 'ultra-libertarian', claimed to be so concerned about regulation that he actually set up a taxpayer-funded inquiry into the 'nanny state'.[5] Yet he also wanted to ban wind turbines because of the 'infrasound' they generate.[6] A genuine libertarian would tell the tiny minority of people who are bothered by the infrasound to sell their houses to members of the vast majority who can't hear it.

Our economy, and indeed our society, literally couldn't function without regulation. While history and international observation tells us that it is possible to create healthy and wealthy societies with an enormous range of regulation, economics cannot actually tell us which regulations are 'best'. Decisions about the kind of regulations we want are ultimately decisions about the kind of society we want. They are expressions of our values and our objectives, and so are best made democratically. That's why business groups work so hard to dress debates about regulation up in econobabble – to ensure those debates aren't democratically inclusive.

Business groups know perfectly well what the answer would be if citizens were asked: 'Do you think factories should be free to pollute our air and water?' Econobabble allows a skilled business lobbyist or politician to reframe the question: 'Keeping in mind the importance of maintaining our competitive advantage, would you support additional regulations on Australian businesses if it resulted in higher costs to producers and consumers?'

REGULATION IS EVERYWHERE, AND THAT'S A GOOD THING

Most people don't want poo on their food. Or cockroaches in commercial kitchens. Or meat that hasn't been kept in a fridge. That's why nearly everybody supports the regulation of the food industry. Everyone except those parts of the food industry that 'keep costs down' by importing the odd bit of food with poo on it. During the COVID-19 crisis, some libertarians argued it was unreasonable to demand staff and customers wear masks in some settings, but it is rare to hear requirements that employees who handle food wear gloves described as an abuse of human rights. Again, there is no 'right' amount of regulation, but it is wrong to suggest that no regulation is a worthy, or achievable, goal.

Car companies are forced to install seat belts in all cars sold in Australia. But the red tape doesn't stop there: we also force people to wear them, and we pay police to check if people are complying. And if they aren't, we force them to pay a fine. In a true 'free market', car companies would choose whether to install seat belts or not, customers would choose whether they wanted to buy cars with seat belts or not, and passengers would decide whether to wear seat belts or not. And in a society free of 'burdensome' regulation, we could all drive on either side of the road – or even the footpath – in cars that lacked not only seat belts but mufflers as well. Such a scenario is obviously ridiculous. In a society that had no taxes or regulation, there would be no roads to drive on anyway.

There is no evidence to support the idea that individuals left to their own devices always make decisions that are in their own best interests, let alone in the community's best interests. Not even Adam Smith, the man who gave us the concept of the 'invisible hand', believed we needed no regulation. Consider the following:

- Should your neighbours be allowed to make as much noise as they want at any time they want? Should they be able to throw their rubbish over your fence?

- Should factories be able to dispose of their untreated pollution into the air or water whenever they want?

- Should shops be able to sell products that fall apart within days of purchase?

- Should food producers be allowed to conceal the ingredients they include in the food they sell?

If you answered 'no' to any of the above questions, then obviously you are a red-tape-loving nanny-statist who wants to stifle innovation and individual responsibility by creating more burdensome regulation. Either that or you're a sensible adult.

A favourite right-wing debating trick is to push people into accepting one of two extreme, and ridiculous, positions. For example, do you think that red tape is ruining the world, or do you think that individuals are better than bureaucrats at deciding how to live their lives? Are you with us or against us?

The best strategy is to respond in kind. Do shock-jocks think we should let hoodlums make as much noise as they want at any time, or should we implement tough laws (regulations) to ensure that hard-working citizens can get some rest at night? (If you haven't noticed, most shock-jocks claim to hate 'nanny-state regulation', but they simultaneously claim to love 'law and order'.)

In reality, regulation is always a compromise. Some regulations are stupid, and some do stifle innovation. But that doesn't stop the taxi industry from demanding regulatory protection from ride-sharing companies like Uber. And it doesn't stop music companies wanting tougher 'laws' to imprison and fine people who share movies or music with their friends. It's not only environmentalists and fussy consumer groups who can be accused of supporting regulations which stifle innovation and competition.

BUSINESSES DON'T WANT TO BE 'COMPETITIVE', THEY WANT TO BE MONOPOLISTS

One of the most shocking conclusions of economic theory is that in an efficient market, firms barely make a profit. That is, when a market is genuinely 'competitive' – in the economists' sense of the word – and has many buyers and sellers, none of whom have market power and all of whom are selling similar products, no individual firm will ever make a large profit.

It gets weirder. In the land of the economics textbook, the land econobabblers pretend to know well, firms earning large profits are a sign that something is *wrong* with the market. Large profits are in fact evidence of 'market failure'. Indeed, economists think that large profits should only ever be a temporary problem, as the profit itself would act as a signal to other firms to enter the market. New entrants, possibly using new technologies, should be able to push prices and profits down, and restore the market to its competitive (low-profit) state (which economists call *equilibrium*).

The way the pursuit of profit destroys profit is a big part of Adam Smith's 'invisible hand', and it's why economists love the idea of 'free markets'. Businesspeople, on the other hand, don't actually like free markets and healthy competition for the same reason that economists do like those things: genuine competition reduces the likelihood of profits.

For a company to maintain high levels of profitability, it needs to be able to prevent new competitors from entering the market. Economists call things that keep new entrants out of a market 'barriers to entry'; businesspeople call them by many names, including:

- licences (the taxi, casino and television industries are built on them);

- patents (Apple tried to keep Samsung out of the tablet computer market by claiming they owned the idea of a rectangular screen);

- copyrights;

- trademarks;

- joint marketing boards (such as the Australian Wheat Board); and

- Geographical Indications (for instance, that champagne can only be produced by winemakers from the Champagne region of France).

While businesses use a wide and contradictory array of econobabble to justify the need for the barriers to entry that protect their profits, they can be summarised with the word the business community is determined not to use: *regulation*.

There is simply no such thing as a 'free market'. Nowhere. For anything. All markets are regulated in some way. Unfortunately, the nonsensical debate about whether we should regulate markets or not is used by the econobabblers to crowd out a more interesting and important conversation about which kinds of regulation are good for society and which kinds are not. While there will be no simple answer to that question, a national debate would likely yield far better outcomes for consumers, citizens, the environment and even the economy. There would probably be losers, too, but in a free market that is exactly what is supposed to happen.

While trained economists assume that profits are a signal for new firms to enter an industry and push prices down for consumers, in Australia profits are used to build barriers to entry to keep competitors out and prices up. And the cheapest and most effective are regulatory barriers. Let's consider some examples.

The taxi industry

Taxis in most Australians capital cities are expensive, slow, unreliable and smelly. They were also, for a long time, very, very profitable. So profitable, in fact, that back in 2011, a licence to own a taxi in Sydney cost around $400,000. That is, to enter the taxi market, a new entrant had to pay an existing taxi operator nearly half a million dollars to overcome the regulatory 'barrier to entry'. But competition from ride-share services like Uber has changed all that.

Since the arrival of ride-sharing services, the price of a Sydney taxi licence had collapsed to 'only' $60,000 in November 2020. To be clear, that's still a big barrier to entry, but not nearly as big as it used to be, for the simple reason that the profits on the other side of the barrier are much smaller than they used to be. Think about that: you have to pay your competitor for the right to compete with them. So much for 'free markets'.

Technological change often overcomes the barriers behind which profitable monopolists and oligopolists hide. Google destroyed the profits of the *Yellow Pages*. eBay destroyed the profitability of classified advertisements. Facebook gobbled up so much of the advertising market that newspapers are collapsing all around the country. And GPS navigation has destroyed the profits of the street directory publishers. But the taxi industry isn't going to go quietly. They can see the barbarians at the regulatory gate, and they are spending enormous amounts of their customers' money to solidify the regulatory barriers that protect their enormous profits.

Hire cars have always provided some competition to taxis, but only when the consumer planned ahead. The bizarre but effective laws that protect the owners of taxi licences specifically prevent 'hire cars' from picking people up off the street. You can only use them if you book in advance. Similarly, paying your mate some 'petrol money' for a lift home has always been legal. But both hire cars and organising for a friend to drive take foresight, which, historically, has left the taxi industry with a monopoly on providing last-minute rides. Technological change now allows us to 'book' an Uber car one minute before we need it, or find a 'friend' online willing to drive us somewhere for money.

Where customers see convenience, the taxi industry sees competition. And when profits are under serious threat, the first thing thrown overboard is the rhetoric of free markets.

As ride-sharing companies like Uber, DiDi and Ola have set up in cities around the world, the owners of Australia's taxis have not responded by making their service cleaner, cheaper or more reliable. Experience tells the taxi industry that the best way to see off competition is to desperately chase stronger regulation that will keep the new competitors out. But of course the explanation the taxi companies give for doing this has nothing to do with their profits – they simply want to 'protect their customers'.

While new entrants have created more competition and a service that millions of customers clearly prefer, they also cause new problems that the 'free market' cannot solve. Ensuring that workers in the gig economy receive fair pay, have a safe work environment and provide a safe service will inevitably require new regulations – regulations which, in turn, may create new barriers to entry, which the current crop of ride-share providers will no doubt support.

The pharmacists

In 2012, two pharmacists proposed opening a new store in the Canberra suburb of Hackett, but it was quickly derided as a crazy idea. Given that there was already a chemist 1.5 kilometres away, in the suburb of Watson, there was clearly no need for a new one in Hackett. Anyone who has read the federal government's 'Pharmacy Agreement' knows that a new pharmacy cannot be opened within 1.5 kilometres of an existing one. Imagine if there were two near each other! Competing! One might even promise not to make you wait for five minutes before they go and get your pills off the shelf. Where will it end?

The Pharmacy Guild of Australia is one of the country's most powerful unions. In fact, it is so powerful that it is considered impolite to call it a union. It's a guild – and don't you forget it.

The pharmacists' union has one of the biggest buildings of all the lobbyists who can afford to have a permanent physical presence in Canberra's very expensive 'Parliamentary Triangle'. You might think it is odd for a

bunch of small-business owners to take Canberra lobbying and the need for 'stable regulation' so seriously, but the
fact is that every Australian pharmacy has a local monopoly
on the distribution of billions of dollars' worth of taxpayer-
subsidised medicine each year. And they are the only people
who can charge $7 for a bag of 'glucose' jelly beans. It's a very
nice little earner.

The regulations banning new shops from setting up
don't just protect pharmacists from competition, they also
ensure that young pharmacists have no choice but to work
for the incumbents rather than set up on their own. One
day, if they are lucky, the young chemists can pay millions
of dollars to buy one of the restricted number of pharmacies, from someone whose business has been protected
from competition for decades. While pharmacies usually
smell a bit better than taxis, the laws that protect them
both stink.

We could 'let the market decide' how many pharmacists an area can support. We could allow supermarkets to
employ trained pharmacists and let them dispense drugs;
this is what happens in most countries. Or we could stick
with the status quo.

The pharmacy industry, like the taxi industry, is adamant that the existing regulations are there to protect
customers, not pharmacy owners. That's a relief.

Free-to-air television

For decades, Australians had access to only three commercial free-to-air television stations because the government had decided to issue only three licences. That, we were told, was the right number. Granting only two licences would not have allowed for enough 'competition', and granting four licences would be unsustainable – and we wouldn't have wanted to see an entrepreneur try to set up a fourth channel and go broke. It's better to protect people from themselves.

As Australia's population grew, and the total advertising revenue of the three commercial television stations grew faster still, it seemed that three remained the right number of channels. Without their big profits, we were told, the commercial television stations couldn't afford to make Australian content. As luck would have it, restricting the number of commercial television licences was the best way to both protect and promote Australian culture.

But then something strange happened. As more and more people began to use mobile phones and wireless internet services, the 'electromagnetic spectrum' in which phone, internet, radio and television signals are broadcast began to get crowded. A partial solution to this congestion was to move television broadcasts to new frequencies, which, when combined with the switch from analogue to digital transmission, meant there was now the possibility of around forty free-to-air television stations.

So what is the right number of free-to-air commercial television licences now? You will never guess: it's still three.

It turned out that, despite our capacity to admit new broadcasters to the Australian television market, the best way to give Australians 'choice' was to let the three owners of the existing licences decide what else we can see. And their decision – which was largely to put more infomercials and repeats to air – speaks volumes.

Commercial television licenses are worth hundreds of millions of dollars. And just like in the taxi industry and the pharmacy industry, if you want to enter the television market you have to pay one of the incumbents for the privilege.

SO DO WE NEED MORE REGULATION OR LESS?

'The challenge is to strike the right balance between appropriate safety standards and consumer access to vehicles at the lowest price. Policy options are still being considered and it is expected the marketplace will play a role in providing consumers with options to mitigate the risks of overseas purchases.'

—**Jamie Briggs, assistant infrastructure and regional development minister, 2015**[7]

Try to decode the above quote. I can't. Despite their rhetoric about deregulation, most free-marketeers, when pushed for their position on regulations that protect the profits of existing companies, head straight for the econobabble. The above quotation, for example, is an attempt by former MP Jamie Briggs to answer the question of whether we should make it easier to import second-hand cars. His reference to 'the marketplace playing a role' was a nice touch, given that the question was whether or not *the parliament* would change the regulations.

To recap, the idea that business owners want truly 'free markets' and open 'competition' is as absurd as it is widely repeated. Regulation is the most powerful weapon in the corporate arsenal, and the purpose of all the money spent by companies on lobbying, PR and political donations is to ensure that, whoever is in government, the regulations that enable their profits are protected and enhanced.

Throughout the 1990s and 2000s, the 'economic rationalists' raged against red tape and regulation. They mounted a noisy and effective campaign opposed to regulation and in support of free markets. It was not an accident that their calls focused on the need to privatise government services and 'deregulate' the labour market. And it was no accident that the need to 'deregulate' pharmacies, taxis and television never appeared on their to-do list.

WHY DIVESTMENT DIVIDES THE RIGHT

Despite their 'libertarian' values when it comes to the corporate world, most conservatives usually abandon the cause of freedom when it comes to our personal lives. Nowhere is the hypocrisy of the political Right more obvious than in the arbitrary line they draw between 'economic issues' and 'social issues'. Indeed, many right-wingers want a government that is just small enough to fit into your bedroom.

Consider the recent controversies around 'divestment'. The divestment movement is a worldwide campaign aimed at encouraging individuals, community organisations, universities, investment funds and companies to sell their shares in businesses that are engaged in activities inconsistent with the shareholders' values. While the most visible divestment campaigns in the world today revolve around concerns about climate change – they encourage the sale of shares in fossil-fuel companies – a wide range of other environmental and human rights campaigns are also being conducted.

Divestment campaigns pose an existential threat to the political compromise between 'market liberals' and 'social conservatives' that defines the modern coalition between the Liberals and Nationals in Australia. Consider the following:

- For decades, market liberals have chosen to focus on the 'deregulation' of markets, but have been largely silent about 'values issues', such as freedoms in relation to homosexual sex, same-sex marriage, euthanasia, abortion or the prohibition of recreational drugs.

- For decades, 'social conservatives' have chosen to focus on 'values issues' related to sexuality, drugs and death, while remaining largely silent about 'social justice' issues such as the gap between rich and poor, the adequacy of the social safety net, and the need for decent wages and conditions.

The business community and conservative churches have spent decades behaving like pharmacists and staying off each other's turf, but now divestment campaigns are bringing the world of money and the world of social values crashing into each other.

Consumers are trained daily to believe that the things they own say something about them. The cars, clothes, perfume and watches we own are all, we are told, a reflection of ourselves. But while many progressives have raged against the idea that 'we are what we own', in recent times campaigners such as Bill McKibben have shifted the public debate, arguing that if we are what we own, we shouldn't own shares in companies which profit from activities that are inconsistent with our values.

The significance of the political and philosophical threat posed by the divestment movement was on full display in the Abbott government's response to the Australian National University's decision to divest itself of a small bundle of shares in mining companies. The education minister and the Minerals Council of Australia raged against the decision. The then prime minister said the decision was 'stupid'.[8]

During the kerfuffle, the Australia Institute took out a full-page advertisement in the *Australian Financial Review*, pointing out:

- that capitalism is built on the notion that shareholders can sell their shares whenever they want; and

- that the government was simultaneously suggesting the leadership of the ANU was making 'stupid' investment decisions, and that (if the government's proposed deregulation of university fees happened) those same 'stupid' people would be setting the prices of university degrees.

While divestment campaigns alone will never be sufficient to tackle climate change, end child labour or ensure gender pay equality, there is little doubt that they can raise awareness of these issues as well as give individuals a way to put their money where their mouth is. They play an important role in 'making room' for regulatory solutions.

If the business and political leaders who claim to have so much faith in freedom and individual choice meant a word of what they said, they would have endorsed the divestment movement for what it is: individuals expressing their desires through the market.

But the words of most business leaders about free markets, individual choice and the power of market forces are just econobabble. They've been carefully selected to mean nothing, and to crowd out real democratic debates about what we should regulate and how we should go about it.

The Myth of Free Trade

Free-trade agreements are the most deceptive and misleading product since the mining industry told the world that 'clean coal' would tackle climate change. The American government is determined to restrict imports of sugar, the Japanese government is determined to restrict imports of rice and the Australian government claims to have free-trade agreements with both of them! And of course, in the middle of the COVID-19 crisis, the Chinese government introduced restrictions on the importation of Australian coal, barley, lobsters and timber – even though we'd signed a 'free trade agreement' with them in 2015, which the then prime minister, Tony Abbott, described as 'a testament to the strength of the Australia–China relationship'.[1]

Despite all the rhetoric, there is no such thing as free trade, and no country on the planet is pursuing free trade as a goal. So-called free-trade agreements are actually nothing of the sort. The document known as the *Australia–United States Free Trade Agreement* is over 1000 pages long, but you should be able to sum it up in one line: 'There will be no restrictions on trade between Australia and the United States.' What those thousand pages in fact do is spell out all the mutually agreeable restrictions on trade between Australia and the United States. As people have gradually caught on to the fact that free-trade agreements are nothing of the sort, governments have tried to rebrand them. Take the Trans-Pacific Partnership, for example. Who could be opposed to a 'partnership'?

Trade isn't good or bad – it is simply trade. All countries impose rules on trade to protect their customers, industries or geopolitical interests. Conservative politicians have created a phoney debate about 'free trade' in order to conceal what they are really up to: redefining the rules of trade in ways that are good for people they like and bad for those they don't like.

WHAT WOULD REAL FREE TRADE LOOK LIKE?

Despite our so-called free-trade agreement with the United States, Australian residents can't download music or movies from US companies on the same terms as American residents – we get them later and at higher prices. The US sellers use 'geo-blocking' software to ensure that

Australian consumers can't freely trade with them. Here are a few examples:

- Apple charges Australian consumers more to download Australian music from iTunes than it charges Americans to purchase the same songs.

- The jeweller Tiffany sells exactly the same pieces to Americans at significant lower prices than they charge Australians. If an Australian goes to the US website and tries to pay the US price, they are redirected to the more expensive Australian website.

- Netflix charges Australians higher prices than it charges US residents, and often cannot make programs available to Australians until months after US residents have seen them.

Those arguing for an Australia–US free trade agreement claimed it would give Australians greater choice at lower prices. But now that the agreement is in place, they're conspicuously silent about the inability of Australian consumers to access these benefits.

NO COUNTRY WANTS FREE TRADE

Like most countries, Australia encourages other nations to embrace free trade, but we are deeply reluctant to do so ourselves. Of course, while other countries are motivated solely by short-sighted and selfish 'protectionism', Australia's trade restrictions have no such base motives. Consider the following:

- We want Japan to abolish its restrictions on importing rice, but we restrict the importing of bananas.

- We want the United States to lift its restrictions on importing our sugar, but we won't allow fresh chicken meat to be imported into Australia.

- We want Indonesia to relax its restrictions on Australian meat, but we plan to keep our extensive restrictions on the importing of second-hand cars.

Fortunately, in my view at least, Australian citizens can't freely import assault rifles from the United States because Australian trade restrictions prevent it. Again, trade isn't good or bad – it's just trade. It's citizens who distinguish good from bad, not economists or trade negotiators. Unfortunately, however, all the econobabble about 'free trade' being 'good for the economy' has stopped us from having a much-needed debate about which restrictions on trade are good and which ones are not.

Australian and US trade negotiators do have conversations about this sort of thing – in private – but the phoney language of 'free trade versus protectionism' keeps the population out of it. Our trade negotiators therefore make all the important decisions without justifying themselves to the people whose interests they supposedly serve.

AMERICANS AREN'T AFRAID OF GUNS, BUT THEY ARE AFRAID OF CHEESE

Americans, as we all know, are a bunch of freedom-loving, risk-taking, rugged individualists whose only fear related to guns is that they don't have enough of them. Americans don't need nanny-state regulations to protect them from armour-piercing bullets. The Constitution gives them all the protection they need . . . but not enough protection from unpasteurised cheese.

Even freedom-loving, risk-taking Americans aren't irresponsible. They might know that guns don't kill people, but they also know that unpasteurised cheese will. And while thousands of kids are killed by guns in the United States each year, one kid dying from listeria from unpasteurised French cheese is, it seems, just too big a risk to take. That's why they ban the importing of raw-milk Camembert, Brie, goat's cheese and a wide range of other dairy products. A cynic might argue that the American dairy industry wants protection from high-quality French imports.

Don't get me wrong – maybe it's a great idea to ban unpasteurised cheese imports. I'm an economist, not an epidemiologist, and I know next to nothing about bacterial infections. But I do know BS when I hear it. And you don't need to be an epidemiologist or an economist to spot the fundamental and glaring inconsistencies in the arguments that are used to support 'free trade' for some things and 'protection' for others.

AMERICANS CAN MAKE CHAMPAGNE, BUT THEY CAN'T SELL IT TO AUSTRALIANS

Australian winemakers once produced champagne, but they are no longer allowed to. The French won't let them, so these days Australian winemakers produce 'sparkling wine'. The use of the term *champagne* provides an interesting example of the tension between two assumptions in the idea of 'perfect competition', upon which so much policy is based.

One assumption is that of 'perfect information'. To put it another way, it's assumed that consumers always know what they are buying and so can never be ripped off. It's a pretty heroic assumption to make. Clear labelling laws can help consumers, so insisting that only wineries in the Champagne region can sell champagne is, arguably, a pro-consumer attempt to make sure people know what they are buying.

However, another of the assumptions that underpin the belief in free markets says that 'there are no barriers to entry'. What this means is that there is nothing that will stop new wineries (or factories or anything else) from supplying similar products.

So we have two competing priorities – consumer protection and free trade – and weighing them is a highly political and subjective exercise. What's more, the decisions are made by politicians who are usually under a lot of pressure from an industry lobbyist or seven. History suggests that politicians would much prefer to conduct such balancing acts behind closed doors – perhaps because the ultimate decision usually has far more to do with bargaining and lobbying power than it does with economic efficiency or consumer protection.

Now, are you ready for your head to explode? Did you know that although Australian winemakers aren't allowed to make champagne because they aren't from the Champagne region of France, Californian winemakers are? The reason is simply that America has a lot more bargaining power than Australia.

The US market is a lot more important to French wine exporters than the Australian market is, and the French didn't want to get into a trade war with the United States. What the French saw as 'matters of principle' when negotiating with Australia became 'matters of market size' when dealing with the Americans.

The idea that some product names can only be used by producers from a particular region is known in trade law circles as Geographical Indication (GI). It effectively creates a brand that can only be used by producers who come from a particular area. Everyone knows about wine regions such as Champagne and Bordeaux, but other examples include Stilton and Roquefort cheese. It seems simple, but in fact it's not.

We know that Australia has a 'free-trade agreement' with the United States, which is supposed to mean that there are no restrictions on trade between our two countries. And we now know that while American winemakers can call their sparkling wine *champagne*, Australian winemakers can't. So can an American winemaker export its champagne to Australia? No chance. The 'free-trade agreement' between the United States and the European Union specifically bans US companies from exporting anything called *champagne* to Australia.

It gets worse. Deals between individual countries are called 'bilateral' agreements while those among multiple countries are called 'multilateral' agreements – examples of the latter are the North American Free Trade Agreement and the Trans-Pacific Partnership. Not only do rules in some bilateral deals override rules in some multilateral deals, but sometimes rules in multilateral agreements can override rules in bilateral agreements.

There is nothing 'free' about the interlocking set of bilateral and multilateral trade agreements that regulate trade between countries. Indeed, companies that can't afford teams of lawyers to help them navigate the overlapping regulatory nets have no chance of competing with those companies that can.

Even the 'free marketeers' at the Productivity Commission have been critical of the current approach to trade agreements. It refuses to use the term *free-trade agreements*, preferring the more accurate *preferential-trade agreements*. In a 2015 report it stated: 'Preferential-trade agreements add to the complexity and cost of international trade through substantially different sets of rules of origin, varying coverage of services and potentially costly intellectual property protections, and investor-state dispute settlement provisions.' Five years earlier, it noted that 'businesses have provided little evidence that Australia's [bilateral trade agreements] have generated significant commercial benefits'.[2]

Needless to say, despite the Commission's concerns, neither the bureaucrats at the Department of Trade nor the business groups that usually rage against such bureaucrats have expressed any worry that these agreements are stifling trade for the small businesses that are struggling to navigate the byzantine and overlapping set of rules Australia now has.

SO IF FREE TRADE DOESN'T EXIST, WHY DO SO MANY POWERFUL PEOPLE PRETEND TO WANT IT?

Hitler's propaganda chief, Joseph Goebbels, said that if you're going to tell a lie, you should make it a big one. What we call free-trade agreements are really the exact opposite. The long and complicated deals actually promise to treat some countries, and some industries, differently. To call such an abuse of language 'Orwellian' overstates Orwell's foresight. Free-trade agreements primarily deliver benefits to the industry groups that are powerful enough to shape them. There are three main reasons countries pursue free-trade agreements; let's examine them in turn.

I. Free-trade agreements provide powerful images.

While it may seem trite, a major benefit of signing a free-trade agreement with the United States or China is the photo opportunity that comes with it. The leaders of large and powerful countries know this and use it to their advantage in negotiations. Do you think the US media paid as much attention to signing a free-trade agreement with Australia as the Australian press did? What Australian prime ministers might call a defining moment in our relationship with a powerful country is no more than a footnote in theirs. (Sometimes literally so: George W. Bush's biography made only three passing references to John Howard, including a footnote, while Howard dedicated large slabs of his autobiography to his relationship with Bush.)

While Australian politicians suggest our free-trade agreement with the United States makes us special, in fact the Americans have signed twenty such 'special' agreements with countries as diverse as Honduras, Jordan, Peru and Canada. They're currently pursuing at least thirteen more, in order to strengthen their 'special' relationships with Mozambique, Mauritius and the United Arab Emirates, among others.

2. Free-trade agreements are weapons in the domestic political war.

The opaque nature of trade negotiations allows negotiators enormous latitude to pursue benefits for their political friends and impose pain on industries or constituencies to which they are hostile or indifferent.

For example, despite the fact that agriculture accounts for only 2 per cent of Australia's gross domestic product,[3] access to new agricultural export markets is central to our trade negotiations, and especially when the National Party provides the trade minister, as it usually does when the Coalition is in power. Other industries are barely mentioned.

But while National Party trade ministers are fiercely opposed to free trade in bananas and chicken, they have been far less concerned about protections for the manufacturing industries. There aren't a lot of factories in National Party electorates.

Despite making Australian access to the US sugar market a line-in-the-sand issue, even John Howard's 'special' relationship with George W. Bush wasn't enough to get the United States to agree to something that would harm its heavily protected sugar industry. Like most lines in the sand, Howard's was washed away by the tide of political power, and Australia signed a free-trade agreement with the United States that specifically prevented free trade in sugar. Needless to say, the US sugar industry has remained largely untouched by the twenty free-trade agreements the US government has entered into. It's the same story with the Japanese rice industry, which has been largely unaffected by its government's equally strong commitment to 'free trade'.

The rise of populism in countries like the United States, the United Kingdom and Australia has had a big impact on the rhetoric around free-trade agreements. Take what was known as the Trans-Pacific Partnership, for example. It has evolved into the Comprehensive and Progressive Agreement for Trans-Pacific Partnership. How could anyone have a problem with a deal that is both progressive and a partnership? But while the optics and language might have changed, the underlying strategy for countries like Australia has not: use international agreements to help grow the exports of your friends, while driving 'reform' of the industries and unions of your enemies.

3. Free-trade agreements are about geopolitics.

Free-trade agreements provide a forum in which countries can demonstrate their friendship with (or fealty to) other countries. As the Productivity Commission has observed, 'The characterisation of security and strategic relationships as a central justification for a trade agreement is a cause of some concern, as the practical value of any contribution made by [bilateral and regional trade agreements] to such relationships is often not clear and yet such considerations can seem to dominate other considerations.'

Australian governments, for example, have given Chinese companies the right to bring their own labour, and Chinese wages and conditions, to Australia as they mine our resources and build our infrastructure.[4] Similarly, we have given US companies the right to appeal changes to our laws in international tribunals.[5]

Put simply, modern trade agreements typically require small countries to give up some of their sovereign rights. Evidently, those who have negotiated such deals on our behalf believe that the price we pay is worth it – but if they hold that view so strongly, then why are they so determined to characterise the decisions they make as a choice between 'free trade' and 'protection', rather than between independence and interdependence?

HOW TO CALL OUT THE ECONOBABBLE ABOUT FREE TRADE

Barnaby Joyce didn't want free trade in bananas, John Howard never wanted free trade in guns, and even Cory

Bernardi opposed free trade in drugs. Are there any in the current Coalition government who are committed to the freedom of people to move around the world chasing higher wages in the way the economic models assume?

The only way to win a debate about what the shock-jocks call 'free trade' is to make it clear to everyone that there is no such thing in its absolute form, and that conservative governments have no interest in achieving it. Only after it has been established that every industry and every political party supports the restrictions on trade that they like do you have any chance of winning a debate about the particular restrictions on trade that you prefer.

Democratic countries must make a wide range of judgements about what they think is in their national interest. There are benefits to encouraging trade and there are benefits to restricting trade. Reducing tariffs, quotas and other trade restrictions can drive innovation and efficiency, or it can make it more attractive for companies to shift work offshore to factories where workers are handcuffed to their sewing machines. Removing import restrictions on food can give Australian access to new and cheaper forms of fresh food, or it can allow new diseases to decimate our crops and result in Australians eating berries that have been watered with untreated sewerage.

Neither side of politics makes judgements like these perfectly all of the time, but few Australians even know that such decisions are being made. The extreme language of 'free trade' versus 'protection' conceals the significance of the wide range of decisions that would best be made with a high degree of public and parliamentary scrutiny.

What is really required is a rigorous, and inevitably messy, political debate about which kinds of protections we want to provide to which kinds of industries. But as long as we are having phoney debates about whether free trade is 'good' or 'bad', we can't start the hard discussions about better and worse forms of protection and deregulation.

THE TRUTH COMES OUT

In July 2015, the then trade minister, Andrew Robb, made a surprising admission, when it was put to him that the negotiations for the TPP lacked transparency:

> It's been a bit of a straw man, this issue of confidentiality. We've had over one thousand consultations. There are a range of industry groups at these negotiations, who we talk with every day, as has been the case with every time I've been to any negotiation anywhere in the world. The industry groups are there. It's quite a misnomer to suggest that we haven't contacted or we don't know what people want.[6]

In order to form his position, the minister had over a thousand consultations with industry groups. While unions, environmental groups and academics were prevented from seeing the draft text of the TPP deal, industry groups – the very same groups which publicly call for 'deregulation' and 'free trade' – were given privileged access to the negotiation process.

Two days later, Andrew Robb took up the point again: 'The industry groups from every country, including our own, make some often very ambitious claims. Those that are trying to defend their markets get fairly bullish about it, but this is the whole point of these agreements.'[7]

So there you have it. The 'whole point' of free-trade agreements is so industry groups can defend the regulations that make them money.

The Use and Abuse of Economic Modelling

'There are assumptions in the budget. There are always assumptions in the budget. There are assumptions about many things. But this budget is a plan, and that plan is not dependent on those assumptions.'

—Prime Minister Scott Morrison[1]

Every time you hear a politician or business leader talk about the 4734 jobs that will be lost if we protect the environment, or the $4.673 billion 'cost to the economy' associated with an attempt to protect consumers, you are hearing the result of an economic model, and you should be sceptical. Very sceptical.

While the preceding chapters have considered specific arguments about specific issues, this chapter looks at the use and abuse of a particularly powerful tactic in the econobabblers' repertoire – the use and abuse of economic modelling.

An economic model is to the economy what a slot car is to a racing car. The parts might look similar, but in reality they are totally different things. Joseph Stiglitz once made this very point. 'When I began the study of economics some forty-one years ago,' he said, 'I was struck by the incongruity between the models that I was taught and the world that I had seen growing up.'[2]

While economic modelling has become omnipresent in our public and political debate over the last fifteen years, it is almost entirely invisible in undergraduate economic degrees. Indeed, it is absent from most postgraduate economic studies. Most economists know as much about how the most widely used economic models work as most politicians – and by that I mean virtually nothing.

That doesn't mean that most economists are stupid; it means that economic modelling is something that almost no one understands. Of course, the fact that virtually no one knows what is going on inside the economic models that drive so much of our economic debate makes it the most powerful dialect of the language that is econobabble. What could silence the masses better than a language that only a handful of Australians speak?

Bizarrely, while the transparent and evidence-based modelling conducted by climate scientists has been widely criticised by those who profit from causing climate change, the top-secret and assumption-based economic modelling sold by a handful of economic consulting businesses in Australia is typically accepted uncritically by journalists, bureaucrats and senior politicians as objective truth.

The problem with most of the economic modelling used in public debate is that it is complete rubbish. The old adage in any form of modelling is 'garbage in, garbage out'. And while good modellers in most disciplines are quite open and transparent about the assumptions they make, most modelling in economics is conducted on the basis that the assumptions are 'commercial-in-confidence'. Indeed, a debate about the impact of increasing the GST reached a state of high farce in July 2015 when the lobby group Chartered Accountants Australia and New Zealand 'released' economic modelling which 'showed' that increasing the GST to 15 per cent would collect an additional $256 billion.[3] The reason that the words *released* and *showed* need to be placed in quote marks is that not only did the accountants refuse to detail the assumptions on which their modelling was based, they also refused to release either the results or the name of the firm that conducted the economic modelling! They claimed that all these highly relevant details were 'commercial-in-confidence', despite the fact that they gave the headline results of their modelling to a journalist from *The Sydney Morning Herald*, which splashed them all over its front page.

Although not all modelling reports are as dodgy as that 'released' by Chartered Accountants Australia and New Zealand, it's often the case that when you examine the technical appendices in the fat modelling reports – or, better yet, when you can question the modellers under oath in a court of law – the results can be as amusing as they are alarming. Consider the following admissions made by economic modellers when questioned under oath:

- The economist for Adani's Carmichael mine admitted that his model assumed that building an enormous new coal mine would not increase coal supply.[4]

- The economist for Yancoal's Ashton mine said that building new mines was 'not about jobs' and that this mine could increase retail wages.[5]

WHAT IS AN ECONOMIC MODEL?

For many people, economic modelling has become fundamental to 'serious policy debate'. People armed with economic modelling are often taken more seriously than those with twenty years' experience working on the same problem. The modelling result that suggests tens of thousands of jobs will be lost or created often trumps logic or experience that suggests such claims are nonsensical.

A model is a simplified representation of a more complex mechanism – and this is true of both slot cars and economics. A model is typically smaller, simpler and easier to build than the full-scale item. A model's main purpose is to illustrate the main features of the reality that it seeks to represent.

An economic model, of course, is not a physical thing like a model car. Rather, it is a mathematical representation of the linkages between the parts of the economy the modeller thinks are important. For example, an economic model of the link between economic growth and taxation would usually be based on historical data. A simple model might distinguish between the impact on economic growth of income tax, the GST and company profits tax, whereas a more complex model might distinguish between the impact on different types of economic growth (such as growth in exports, growth in consumer spending, growth in business investment) of a wider range of Commonwealth taxes, perhaps including capital gains tax, mining taxes and the fringe benefits tax.

Given that no model will ever be a perfectly accurate predictor, and that no model will cope well with unexpected events like the global financial crisis or the arrival of COVID-19, the design of the models used by different organisations is determined by the use to which they are put. For example, a model designed to shed light on the budget deficit or surplus for the following year will likely have less detail but a greater capacity to predict the budget result than a model designed by an investment firm to estimate the amount of tax likely to be paid by individual mining companies.

Put simply, no model can capture the complexity of the entire Australian economy. No model can accurately predict the economic impact of something that has never happened before. And no model is free from a large number of assumptions, which, in reality, are often little more than somebody's best guess.

Honest modellers are humble about what their model can and can't do. They are transparent about the assumptions they have made, and they present their results in a way that minimises the chance that they will be misinterpreted. Well-paid modellers, on the other hand, make bold claims about what their model can do. They use higher-order econobabble to discourage most economists from pressing them very hard about the assumptions they have made and, when pushed, they simply refuse to reveal them.

If science is the process of allowing others to test your hypothesis by following the same steps you have taken, then there is nothing scientific about most commercial economic modelling in Australia.

TRUST ME, I'M AN ECONOMIC MODELLER

The economic modeller's best trick is to imply accuracy by using precision. When someone states that a carbon price will cause the mining industry to lose precisely 23,510 jobs, we don't imagine they could be bluffing. But they are.

In reality, economic modellers use this combination of highly precise predictions and a refusal to explain how their models work to create a mystique around their work: mere mortals fear to question them, let alone lampoon their results. The scientists doing climate modelling should take a closer look at what the economists are getting away with.

Thanks to economic modelling, we know, for instance, that the Melbourne Grand Prix generates tens of millions of dollars' worth of 'economic benefits'. (Of course, we ignore the costs of the noise pollution it generates and the inconvenience it causes Melbourne's residents.) We also know that causing climate change and allowing duck hunting will 'create jobs'.

Buried in all such results are assumptions about the value of your time, the value of peace and quiet or the value of the natural environment (usually zero – but that's an assumption). Such assumptions are of course highly significant, yet those spruiking the models are rarely, if ever, asked about them.

It's even possible to put a value on a human life. People often think that it's difficult, if not impossible, to do this, but in fact it's easy. The hard part is putting an *accurate* value on human life, but if you write enough reports that are sufficiently hard to understand, no one will ask you a simple question like: 'How on earth did you value the life of a child?'

In 2008, a Department of Finance report entitled 'Establishing a Monetary Value for Lives Saved: Issues and Controversies' valued an Australian human life at $151,000 per year.[6] That said, individual departments, consultants and lobbyists are free to use their own assumptions. Of course, citizens are also free to pore over the modellers' thick reports looking for such assumptions, but few do. You might argue that it is the public, or its representatives in parliament, who should weigh up such 'life and death' matters. But while the Australian parliament has held inquiries into everything from the effectiveness of beef marketing to whether wind turbines cause 'wind turbine syndrome', no Australian parliament has ever held an inquiry into the value of a human life, as used when making policy decisions.

While the United States has never held such an inquiry either, Congress has made it clear how it does *not* want human life to be valued. Back in 2003, the US Environmental Protection Agency flirted with changing the way it valued human life, in order to recognise the fact that many economists think the life of an old and sick person is not worth as much as the life of a young and healthy person.[7] The flirting didn't last long. Here's what happened.

Until the early 2000s, the EPA had valued all American lives equally when conducting so-called cost–benefit analyses of policy changes. Then it began experimenting with discounting the value of some lives. Given that air pollution generally kills the old and the sick, the consequences of devaluing the lives of the elderly were highly significant. By assuming that the old and the sick weren't worth as much as an average American, it became harder to show that the benefits to the population of tougher air-pollution regulations were greater than the cost of tougher regulation of the car companies. Put simply, the EPA's 'pensioner discount' assumption could have saved air polluters a lot of money.

Not surprisingly, once the public realised that economists were devaluing their grandmothers' lives, they got interested. Congress eventually passed a bill banning federal government funding for research that discounted the value of retirees' lives.

While the veil of econobabble was in place and the debate focused on 'cost–benefit analyses', 'discount rates' and 'morbidity rates', US citizens were happy to leave 'life and death' issues to the economists and their models. But when the econobabble was stripped away, and the public caught a glimpse of the way in which economists were making their decisions, things changed quickly.

ECONOMISTS KNOW THE PRICE OF EVERYTHING AND THE VALUE OF NOTHING

Economists have a wide range of techniques for attempting to value goods and services that are not bought and sold in markets. These techniques allow economists to *estimate* the 'value' of fresh air or clean water, or of protecting an endangered species or mitigating climate change.

While all such estimates are based on a wide range of assumptions – many of which non-economists find highly implausible – it is important to note that economists don't even know how to accurately value a house, a car, a bottle of water or a song. Economists, like philosophers before them, have spent centuries arguing about what *value* is and how to measure it. Is the value of something based on its usefulness, its necessity, its scarcity or the amount of effort that went into its construction?

Consider this: if we can't live without water, and if we have no real *need* for diamonds, why are diamonds so much more valuable than water? If your answer is that scarcity determines value, then why aren't endangered species worth spending a fortune to protect?

Some people think that goods are more 'real', and thus more 'valuable', than services. Such thinking implies that making musical instruments generates more value than playing them. But if playing an instrument isn't valuable, then what's the point in making them?

People sometimes think that the *price* of something is the same as its *value*. But if that's the case, then how can identical things have different values? As we saw in an earlier chapter, it costs an Australian more to download a song from iTunes than it costs a US citizen – is the song inherently worth more in Australia?

After hundreds of years arguing about what value really means, most economists from the 1950s onwards made a strategic decision to simply work on the assumption that price and value were one and the same thing. While this assumption made no philosophical sense, it did make it much easier for economists to conduct analysis of the enormous quantity of price data floating around.

In more recent decades, however, economists have moved well past any nagging doubts that price and value might not be the same thing, and now assume that we can place a value on human life, human pain and suffering, species extinction and global climate change by asking people how much they would be 'willing and able to pay' to avoid a particular outcome.

The ethical consequences of assuming that the life of a rich person is worth far more than the life of a poor person (because a rich person would be 'willing and able to pay' more for life-lengthening services) are neatly summarised in a memo written by the former chief economist of the World Bank, Lawrence Summers. While the 'Summers Memo', as it is now known, is claimed by its author to have been 'sarcastic', a close reading and a little translation provides a window onto the values and the fundamental limitations of economic modelling.

The Summers Memo
'Dirty' Industries: Just between you and me,
shouldn't the World Bank be encouraging MORE
migration of the dirty industries to the LDCs

[Least Developed Countries]? I can think of three reasons:

The measurements of the costs of health impairing pollution depends on the foregone earnings from increased morbidity and mortality. From this point of view a given amount of health impairing pollution should be done in the country with the lowest cost, which will be the country with the lowest wages. I think the economic logic behind dumping a load of toxic waste in the lowest wage country is impeccable and we should face up to that.

Translation: we value human life based on lost earnings. From this point of view, pollution should occur in poor countries, as the people it kills there are worth less than people in rich countries.

The costs of pollution are likely to be non-linear as the initial increments of pollution probably have very low cost. I've always thought that under-populated countries in Africa are vastly UNDER-polluted, their air quality is probably vastly inefficiently low compared to Los Angeles or Mexico City. Only the lamentable facts that so much pollution is generated by non-tradable industries (transport, electrical generation) and that the unit transport costs of solid

waste are so high prevent world welfare enhancing
trade in air pollution and waste.

Translation: just as a drop of hot water won't harm you but
a cup of hot water can burn you badly, the amount of harm
pollution does rises faster than the 'dose' of pollution to
which a person is exposed. I've always thought that under-
populated countries in Africa are vastly under-polluted,
and that they don't have enough pollution compared with
Los Angeles or Mexico City. It's a pity that so much air
pollution is caused by industries such as transport and
electricity generation, because otherwise we would be able
to make the world a better place by shifting a lot of the pol-
luting activities to the under-polluted developing countries
that have low-value human lives.

The demand for a clean environment for aesthetic
and health reasons is likely to have very high
income elasticity. The concern over an agent that
causes a one in a million change in the odds of
prostrate [*sic*] cancer is obviously going to be much
higher in a country where people survive to get
prostrate [*sic*] cancer than in a country where under
5 mortality is 200 per thousand. Also, much of
the concern over industrial atmosphere discharge
is about visibility impairing particulates. These
discharges may have very little direct health impact.

> Clearly trade in goods that embody aesthetic
> pollution concerns could be welfare enhancing.
> While production is mobile the consumption of
> pretty air is a non-tradable.

Translation: rich people would be willing to pay a lot more money for a healthy and attractive physical environment. Indeed, poor people who are likely to die young from preventable disease probably won't even live long enough to get the cancers caused by many pollutants, so we might as well pollute them anyway. Also, a lot of the concern about particulate pollution is for aesthetic rather than health reasons. It would be great if rich people could pay to move the unattractive pollution to a poor country, because you can produce pollution anywhere but you can only enjoy pretty air where you are right now.

> The problem with the arguments against all of these
> proposals for more pollution in LDCs (intrinsic
> rights to certain goods, moral reasons, social
> concerns, lack of adequate markets, etc.) could be
> turned around and used more or less effectively
> against every Bank proposal for liberalization.

Translation: the World Bank has been making decisions that are good for rich people and bad for poor people since we were set up.

Of course, the fact economists can plug 'GDP per capita' or 'average wages' into their models as a proxy for the value of human life doesn't mean they should. By definition, when a country experiences a recession its GDP falls, and so therefore does its GDP per capita. Did American lives become less valuable during the global financial crisis?

And remember that GDP only captures 'market production' and ignores 'household production'. For example, a parent providing childcare to their own child contributes nothing to GDP, while a parent who pays someone else to care for their child increases GDP. Are the lives of people who care for their own children worth less than those who pay others to do it?

About ten years ago, a lawyer rang me to ask if I would do some (economic) modelling. 'It depends,' I said. 'What's the job?'

'We want you to put a dollar value on the life of a dead mother,' said the lawyer. 'We are suing a doctor for medical negligence, and the insurance company wants to value her life at zero because she wasn't working. She had no future earning potential. Can you estimate the value of the housework she would have performed?'

I still feel sad when I think about it: for the family, for myself, and for a society in which asking such a question is not only acceptable but also necessary. The dilemma for the widower and the lawyer, and for me, was that if someone didn't put a dollar value on the love and care that a mother gives her children, the father would wind up with even less money to care for the kids he would be bringing up by himself.

Of course, economists have no real way to value love and affection, so I valued ironing, laundry and childcare instead. I got my hands on data about how mothers with three kids use their time. I found data on the price of buying individual household services like ironing, and the price of live-in maids and nannies. I forecast the age at which the kids would leave home. My forecast was based on a meaningless average of kids who do go to uni and kids who don't. My spreadsheets were huge, complex, scrupulously referenced and entirely meaningless. Like all good forecasters, I estimated the 'value' of the dead woman's life to the cent, and as happens in all good negotiations, the lawyers ultimately settled for a nice round number. The only good thing about the number was that it was bigger than zero.

This applies at a societal level too. One of the major benefits of tackling climate change is that a lot of lives will be saved. But what are those lives worth? When politicians and economists say that the costs of tackling climate change are greater than the benefits of doing so, they are not making a statement about the economy; they are making a statement about the value of human lives.

Democracies have to find ways to make hard decisions, such as:

- Should we pay more tax and have higher-quality health services?

- Should the government subsidise expensive new drugs, even if they only lengthen the lives of those suffering from rare illnesses for a few months?

- Should seeing a doctor when we feel sick be free to the patient, or should the 'user' pay?

- Should we tackle climate change, or should we just see how things pan out?

Different people, and different countries, have entirely different views about such questions. While the answers have financial and economic consequences, the questions are fundamentally ethical ones. It is a sad fact that the main purpose of economic modelling in Australian public debate is to conceal the ethical dimension of significant policy questions. Having been well paid to make assumptions about the value of human life, the value of avoiding illness and the future value of increased investment in education, many economic modellers now refuse to reveal what those assumptions are, preferring only to focus on the 'answers' their models generate.

If you could bring yourself to read economic modelling reports carefully, you'd be rewarded with some good laughs. For example, you would discover that the economic modelling used to predict the impact of the carbon price on the

Australian economy assumed that, as the carbon price rose, the volume of farts per sheep per year would decline.[8]

It isn't too much to say that almost no one outside the companies selling such nonsense to governments knows about the assumptions on which the models are built. That is why the models are so powerful! Garbage in, garbage out.

CONCLUSION

When done well, economic modelling can provide insights into the more and less obvious linkages between a change to one part of the economy and the impact in other parts of the economy. When used cautiously by informed adults who understand the limitations of what they are doing, modelling can be perceptive and illuminating.

Or it can be used to dress up self-interest as the national interest. When well-paid economic modellers team up with the PR industry on behalf of lobby groups with lots of money, economic models can unleash a flood of econobabble – nonsense that is incomprehensible to most economists, let alone to most voters.

While such a torrent might be impossible to stop, it can be diverted. Journalists, and indeed all citizens, should be asking some simple questions about the economic models used by politicians and lobbyists, and they should demand simple answers in response. As the debacle of the JobKeeper modelling showed, no matter how experienced the modeller, or how important the issue, modellers can get things spectacularly wrong. Treasury's first estimate of the cost of the central plank of the Morrison government's stimulus package was out by $60 billion. $60 billion! Whoops.

No economist knows what the future will look like. Just as no economist in the year 2000 could have imagined what a smartphone would be capable of eight years later, no economist has any idea what new inventions or ideas might arise in the coming decade. And if economists can't even imagine such advances, how on earth can they model their likely impact?

Economic modelling doesn't have to be crap. It doesn't have to be misleading, and it doesn't have to stifle democratic debate. Good modellers are always humble about the limits of their assumptions, and happy to answer questions about the limitations of their assumptions and their model. And always remember, if the person spruiking the modelling can't or won't answer a question about their assumptions, then either they don't know what they're talking about or they are trying to deceive you – it's as simple as that.

What Can Be Done?

Democracies use words, not guns, to resolve disputes. And econobabble can be a powerful weapon. In the public contest of ideas, words can illuminate and lead to improvements in our lives, or they can insult our intelligence, silence citizens, limit the menu of policy options we can consider and fundamentally harm our democracy.

The wall of sound made by the econobabblers drowns out genuine conversation. It creates a cloak, behind which the real objectives of those with powerful voices can hide. Put simply, econobabble helps powerful groups hide the fact that they are getting what they want. Honest economics can help society understand the choices and trade-offs we face, but econobabble conceals most options and disparages most of those that remain. It is central to convincing the public that 'there is no alternative'.

The idea that 'the markets will punish us' if we pursue the social and environmental goals that a majority of Australians want has destroyed much of the ambition in our nation's political debate. But it is not just progressive political parties that self-censor in order to avoid the ridicule of those who 'understand what the market needs'. Unions, non-government organisations, think tanks and individuals often embrace the language of their oppressors and, in so doing, reinforce the belief that 'everyone knows' that 'we can't afford' to provide the level of services that we could afford to provide a generation ago, when our GDP was much smaller.

This book rests on two main premises. The first is that there are no good economic reasons that Australia cannot collect more tax revenue and spend more money on health, education and community services, or use regulation to ensure that 'market outcomes' do not come at the expense of our values, our vision for the future or the natural environment.

The second premise, which perhaps is more important, is that a significant number of Australians aspire to live in such a society. History tells us that it is possible for a small country to develop innovative social policies that have never been tried elsewhere. And international observation tells us that a wide range of countries with lower levels of national income than ours have succeeded in providing far higher levels of health, education, housing and transport services to their citizens than we do. If we want a different country, we can certainly afford it.

But despite the overwhelming public support for closing tax loopholes and spending more money on better health and education, it doesn't happen. This is clearly not a failure to sell 'a vision'; it is a failure to convince people that we can pursue that vision without 'wrecking the economy' or 'making the markets angry'.

There is no need to run a PR campaign about the benefits of investing in health, education or the protection of the environment – the public are already convinced. The problem is not a lack of support for 'the product'; it is the ability of the econobabblers to exaggerate 'the price'.

So what should those who want a better country do if they want to win a debate with the econobabblers, and with the rest of their fellow Australians, about the desirability and the affordability of the society they want? Let's start with the don'ts.

I. Don't accept the premise that we can't afford a better society – they don't.

Australians are, on average, among the richest people ever to live on the earth. While poverty exists in Australia, collectively we control sufficient resources that we can solve any problem we wish to solve. Of course, we can't afford to solve *every* problem that we want. Choosing which problems to solve and which problems to ignore is where democracy, public debate and econobabble come into their own.

Saying that we 'can't afford' to do something sounds a lot nicer than saying that we 'don't want' to do it. Imagine if a prime minster said, 'I don't want to improve the quality of aged care. I'd rather provide tax cuts to high-income earners.' Of course, it'd be much easier and less controversial (if dishonest) for the PM to say, 'We need to cut taxes in order to provide an incentive for people to work hard, so that in the future, once we get the budget under control, we can responsibly invest in higher-quality aged-care services.' Econobabble helps conceal that such a prime minister is making a choice about which group is favoured first.

Those who want to invest more in public services must never accept the premise that the Australian government cannot afford to do something. Conservatives never do. They never argue that money spent on fighter jets, gas pipelines or tax cuts for high-income earners is 'unsustainable' or 'unaffordable'. Those words are reserved for the things they don't want to spend money on – like the aged pension.

2. Don't accept their stated goal of maximising economic growth – they don't.

Conservatives always say that the goal of their policies is 'economic growth' for Australia. But economic growth is a means to an end, not an end in itself. Economic growth is usually measured as the rate of growth in gross domestic product (GDP), which really just means the amount of stuff that was bought and sold in a given year. GDP is an important indicator, especially if you want to know about the volume of stuff being produced, but the idea that simply increasing GDP should be our major objective is so silly that not even the conservatives believe it.

Virtually every economist would argue that investing in high-quality education is a great way to increase economic growth in the long run, yet virtually every conservative government wants to cut spending on public education. If they were serious about increasing GDP, then conservatives would be enthusiastic about investing in education for the entire population. But they aren't, so they don't. What they are serious about is cutting public spending, so that they can cut taxes for the rich.

Similarly, if conservatives truly wanted to increase GDP, then they would be keen to provide low-cost, high-quality childcare to parents who wanted to re-enter the labour force after having a child. There is no more effective way of increasing the proportion of the population in work than to help young parents re-enter the labour market when they are ready to – and, at the beginning of the COVID-19 crisis, that is exactly what the Morrison government did when they made childcare free. Think about that: during nearly thirty years of continuous economic growth, we were told we couldn't possibly afford to provide free childcare, and then, in the middle of the deepest recession in modern history, we could. Of course, it was too good to last, and the Morrison government then repealed this efficient, equitable and effective labour market policy on the basis it was too expensive to maintain . . . And then they brought forward expensive, and permanent, income tax cuts for high-income earners.

As with most problems, however, conservatives prefer to argue that offering tax cuts to high-income earners who already work is a better way to stimulate labour force participation than providing the kind of widespread free childcare provided in France for decades, and in Australia for a few months.[1]

Progressives are often so busy pointing out (quite rightly) that GDP is not the 'be-all and end-all' that they don't notice that conservatives actually agree with them. By pretending to care about GDP, conservative econobabblers can say things like: 'We need tax reform to provide incentives that will kick-start the economy.' What they really mean is: 'I'd like to cut taxes for the wealthy instead of helping get more parents back into the labour force.' Econobabble is much more polite than the truth.

3. Don't fall for false choices – they were invented to make your life a misery.

If you had three kids who were slipping off a cliff and only two hands to grab them with, which of your children would you let die? Kids love asking parents questions like that, and most parents find a way of refusing to answer. It's easy to think up some political questions that most people can't or won't answer:

- Should we spend more money on sick kids or on improving the lives of the elderly?

- Should we invest in new schools or new hospitals?

- Should we protect old-growth forests or throw forestry workers on the scrap heap?

- Should we tackle climate change or help lift people in India out of poverty by giving them access to 'cheap electricity'?

Creating a phoney dilemma is the central political strategy of the modern conservative. It works because progressives often care about helping people *and* about protecting the environment. Making progressives 'choose' between which vulnerable groups to help, or between helping people and protecting the environment, diminishes the enthusiasm of the individuals fighting for simple causes and makes it harder for organisations (such as unions and environmental groups) to work together. Conservatives rarely get caught up in dilemmas about which group to help; their default position is to cut taxes as much as possible and let everyone who isn't rich look after themselves.

The only effective way to respond to a false dilemma is to reject the premise that we can't afford to help multiple groups. We don't have to make such choices if we collect more tax revenue, and we can do that by closing the loopholes that help only the rich. Similarly, progressives must flatly reject the premise that the best way to create jobs is to destroy the environment. The data is quite clear that investment in health and education leads to employment of far more people than investment in mining or forestry.

4. Don't use their objectives to validate your own.

Conservatives don't really prioritise reducing the budget deficit. If they did, then they would be happy to close the tax loopholes from which they benefit; the Treasury would collect tens of billions of dollars more per year in revenue. And, as we've seen, conservatives don't really think GDP growth is the nation's top priority. Given a choice between investments in education (which will enhance productivity) and defence spending (which won't), they will take defence spending any day.

Unfortunately, many progressive organisations have come to believe the econobabble and have distorted their own language so that they fit in with the 'accepted wisdom'. This can result in community organisations accepting (and therefore validating) the existence of a 'budget emergency' and an 'ageing crisis', and accepting cuts to health services.

Or it can result in environmental groups arguing that nature should be protected for its economic benefits. But neither of these topics should be decided by reference to economics alone.

The main reason we should spend more money on preventive health is that it helps people avoid needless pain and suffering. It is a good idea. It is wrong to withhold treatment from vulnerable groups when we know the long-term consequences of this. The fact that well-designed preventive health measures can save our nation a lot of money down the track is a bonus – it's not the main reason we should invest in them. Should parents only vaccinate their kids if the cost of the vaccination is lower than the cost of treating the illness? Or do most parents want to spare their kids unnecessary pain and suffering?

Similarly, the main reason we should protect old-growth forests from clear-felling is that once such ecosystems are destroyed, we will never see their like again. In Tasmania today there is logging proposed in one of the last known nesting sites of the endangered swift parrot. Once it's extinct, we will never see it again. Those who want to protect these remaining wild places because they think it is right to do so, and because they want their kids and their grandkids to have the chance to see them, should say so boldly. The fact that tourism creates far more jobs than the forestry industry (7 per cent of Tasmania's jobs are in tourism, versus less than 1 per cent in forestry) is a bonus, but it should never be the central argument.[2] If the world price of woodchips soared and tourists decided that casinos were more fun to visit than grand forests, should environmentalists abandon their efforts to save the forests?

The economic arguments for good social and environmental policy should only ever play a supporting role in how we advocate for them. To do otherwise accepts the false premise that the GDP growth and budget surpluses should be our ultimate goal, and leaves the advocates vulnerable whenever market prices shift.

5. Don't stay out of economic debates – they matter.

Perhaps the biggest mistake made by many progressives is to stay out of the economic debate on the basis that 'economics is crap' or that it's a mistake to 'engage in their frame'. Whatever the reason, the consequence of staying out of major debates about 'the budget' and 'the economy' is that it cedes to the econobabblers the high ground of Australian public debate.

Conservatives rarely deign to debate the specifics of why we shouldn't have a childcare system as good as France's, a public health system as good as England's or a public transport system as good as New York's. Why bother with actual debate when you can simply argue that 'we can't afford it'?

The idea that progressives can't win when they are talking about the economy has no basis in Australian history. During Labor's longest postwar stint in office, the Hawke and Keating governments drove, and dominated, the national economic debate.

Budgets spell out a government's priorities, and these reflect a society's priorities. It is inconceivable that progressives can reshape our nation without reshaping Commonwealth and state budgets. Similarly, government policies drive the shape of economic growth. While much is made by progressives of the limitations of economic growth as an indicator of progress, it is hard to imagine an environmental group that is indifferent to the question of whether we should be building more coal mines or more wind turbines. Similarly, it is hard to imagine a health group that is indifferent to the question of whether we should be investing more in roads or in hospitals. The simplistic debate about whether economic growth is 'good' or 'bad' prevents progressives from engaging in a genuine conversation about which parts of the economy they want to grow, and which parts they want to decline.

*

Enough with the don'ts. What should those who are sick of having their public debate starved of oxygen by the econobabblers actually do?

I. Do call out the bullshit every time you hear it.

You can't influence a debate unless you're in it. Yelling at the television, moaning to your friends, convincing yourself that no one pays attention to the 'mainstream media' or having a phone hook-up with aggrieved folk from other NGOs does nothing to counter the lies told by the econobabblers or to shift the debate. Debates can only ever be won by those who participate in them.

It's true that no one person, or no one organisation, can successfully break through the wall of sound created by the econobabblers. But when climate sceptics use that argument to justify inaction on climate change, most progressives become livid. Yes, an individual has little power to reshape a national debate – but tens of thousands of determined people definitely can.

You (and anyone else) can …

- phone a radio station to call out BS when you hear it;

- write a letter to the editor of a newspaper;

- post a polite but mocking tweet or Facebook message to inform and empower your friends (#econobabble); and

- write to individual politicians and businesspeople to let them know that you see through the absurdity of their comments.

And of course you can encourage your friends to do the same. Organisations and community groups also can do all of the above. As well, they can ...

- organise events to inform their members about the need to take on the econobabblers and the benefits of doing so;

- change the way they communicate to ensure that they aren't inadvertently reinforcing the power of econobabble; and

- organise, or participate in, public debates about important economic issues.

2. Do sell the big picture by selling the small picture, and sell the small picture by selling the big picture.

The world changes all the time. Our world today barely resembles the world of 100 years ago. And there is no doubt that the world in 100 years' time will be fundamentally different again. The only thing that is certain is that, by then, the politicians, policies and politics of today will all have been washed away.

Given that the world will change, and change radically, all democratic fights are really fights about the direction and pace of *change*. This should provide a big advantage to progressives, who should want change, because of course conservatives should want to leave things as they are. But it doesn't provide that advantage, partly because these days the words *progressive* and *conservative* are more like team names than statements of philosophy. Progressives often want to conserve things (usually elements of the natural environment), while conservatives usually want to change things (especially in relation to the nature of work and, bizarrely, the world's climate).

But philosophical labels aside, there is no doubt that many progressives get confused about whether they should be fighting 'big battles', like tackling world poverty, or 'small problems', like building community resilience and encouraging street gardening. This is, of course, a phoney dilemma.

The world is changed not by global consensus but by the pressure of actions at a range of levels. If absolutely everyone stopped hunting rhinos, all rhinos would be safe from hunting. But what if we can't get everyone to agree to that? Well, if enough individuals declare their hostility to rhino hunting, it becomes politically possible to ban it. Individual actions help deliver political actions. The fossil-fuel divestment campaign is powerful for exactly this reason.

Individuals campaigning for better funding for their local school can simultaneously use their local campaign to raise awareness about the need for governments to invest more in all schools. National organisations calling for greater Commonwealth funding for all schools can simultaneously call for a better tax system that enables government to improve the quality of all public services. Specific examples help sell general propositions, and general propositions help explain the importance of individual changes. It's not either/or – it's both.

3. Do take the high ground and engage in debates.

Anyone who is serious about achieving a significant increase in public investment in health, education or public transport needs to be just as serious about the bigger-picture issues of tax policy, fiscal policy and economic management. Just as *MasterChef* contestants who are 'passionate about their food' but uninterested in the realities of running a small business are unlikely to serve many customers in the long run, so progressives who are passionate about improving the health system but bored by talk of budgets are unlikely to achieve significant change.

People who care deeply about spending need to care deeply about revenue too. Conservative econobabblers rarely argue that money spent on the sick or on school kids is 'wasted'. They simply argue that 'we can't afford it'. The Right does not run campaigns to convince the public that we should spend less on public schools; they campaign to cut taxes, knowing that the less we collect in tax, the less we will spend on schools.

Similarly, groups that want to win fights about work-place or environmental protection laws need to be engaged in bigger-picture debates about the role of regulation in general. Just as those from the Right use general fights about tax to win specific fights about spending, they also use big-picture fights about 'red tape' and 'nanny states' to win specific fights about particular industrial relations or environmental regulations.

If progressive organisations stay out of 'theoretical' or 'ideological' battles about the role of regulation in society, they cede the high ground. When it comes time to push for, or protect, a specific regulation, they have to fight uphill. And the lesson of the last twenty years is that they usually lose.

4. Do work with others outside your 'silo' – you are not always your own best spokesperson.

Many individuals and organisations have no interest in participating in debates about which they are not 'passion-ate', even if they generally support the cause. Fair enough. They don't have to engage in the debate personally – they can empower others to do so on their behalf.

Business groups often organise in such a way that individual companies are spared the effort, or indeed the embarrassment, of calling for the major reforms they want. For example, the Business Council of Australia has waged a twenty-year battle, on behalf of its members, to lower the company tax rate and lower the minimum wage. Such an approach spares individual company CEOs, who often earn millions of dollars per year, from having to argue that their low-paid workers should earn even less.

If individual NGOs and unions can't or don't want to take on groups like the BCA, then they need to create or support groups that will. Groups that want to see an increase in public funding for Indigenous health might feel they have little in common with groups that advocate for young people with disabilities. In reality, both lose out when the BCA achieves further cuts in the corporate tax rate, and both would benefit from an overarching campaign to collect more revenue.

But just as the CEO of a big company can leave the battle to lower their workers' wages to their delegate at the BCA, so too can the leaders of diverse community groups leave the details of specific tax debates to others, if they wish.

5. Do use new ideas to build new alliances.

It is often easier to get people to unite around a new idea than to change their minds about an old idea. Unfortunately for progressives, the flood of econobabble that dominates our public debate makes it difficult for new ideas to be taken seriously. Journalists, politicians and even other progressives are often quick to ask what sound like important questions:

- How will this be paid for?

- Have you done any modelling?

- Isn't it better to let the market solve problems like that?

- Haven't people tried to solve this problem and failed before?

Of course policy ideas should be carefully scrutinised, but it is banal to dismiss new ideas on the basis that one of the world's richest countries 'can't afford it' or because a certain ideology insists problems that markets can't solve aren't worth solving. And of course, in the current climate, you can just argue that it would be a much better use of resources than a gas-led recovery.

A FINAL WORD

Those who want to change the world for the better by improving our social and environmental conditions are, at present, fighting an uphill battle against well-funded opponents. Econobabble is the first line of defence used by those resisting changes that are both popular and equitable.

Unfortunately, in the short term at least, those who want the world to notice their one good idea will first have to join the fight against the econobabblers. Until public debate once again takes place in plain English, the vast majority of Australians will continue to believe that 'the markets will be angry' unless we sacrifice the sick, the poor and the environment.

Managing the economy is important. Unemployment devastates lives. Budgets spell out priorities. Trade with other countries matters. The Australian public will only elect people who care about the economy, but you don't need to be an expert to ask simple questions about it. Whenever you hear a politician talking econobabble, just ask them to say it again in English.

If you have listened closely and sought clarification and you still don't understand, then the person moving their lips either doesn't understand or is trying to pull the wool over your eyes. So the next time you hear someone talking econobabble bullshit, call it out for what it is.

Notes

INTRODUCTION

1. 'What if the Fed chief speaks plainly?', *The New York Times*, 28 October 2005.

2. Michelle Grattan, 'Budget to distinguish good and bad debt', *The Mandarin*, 27 April 2017 (www.themandarin.com. au/78211-budget-distinguish-good-bad-debt).

3. 'Scott Morrison on creating jobs, the banking royal commission and the upcoming election', *7.30*, ABC TV (www.abc.net.au/7.30/ scott-morrison-on-creating-more-jobs,-the-banking/10760724).

4. Nordic Policy Centre, 'Tax and Wellbeing: The Impact of Taxation on Economic Wellbeing', The Australia Institute, 6 October 2020 (www. nordicpolicycentre.org.au/tax_and_wellbeing).

CHAPTER 1: THE LANGUAGE OF DECEPTION

1. 'Josh Frydenberg reveals shrinking deficit in budget outcome', *SBS News*, 19 September 2019.

2. See, for example, David Hetherington, *Per Capita Tax Survey 2015: Attitudes towards Taxation and Public Expenditure*, Per Capita, Melbourne, 2015 (https://percapita.org.au/wp-content/ uploads/2018/05/2015-Tax-Survey-1.pdf).

3. Christopher Knaus, 'Pressure for integrity commission builds as poll reveals loss of trust in politics', *The Guardian*, 15 April 2019 (www. theguardian.com/australia-news/2019/apr/15/pressure-for-integrity-commission-builds-as-poll-reveals-loss-of-trust-in-politics).

4.   The Australia Institute, 'Poll: 80% of Australians Support a Federal Integrity Commission with Strong Powers', 15 April 2019 (https:// australiainstitute.org.au/post/poll-80-of-australians-support-a-federal-integrity-commission-with-strong-powers).

5.   See Daniel Hurst, 'Tony Abbott backs away from iron ore inquiry after lobbying by BHP and Rio', *The Guardian*, 19 May 2015 (www. theguardian.com/business/2015/may/19/tony-abbott-backs-away-from-iron-ore-inquiry-after-lobbying-by-bhp-and-rio).

6.   For WA's shortage of dialysis machines, see Erin Parke, 'Kimberley kidney health breakthrough means residents no longer choose between staying home or saving their lives', *ABC News*, 7 June 2020; for the high cost of shark culling, see 'The Economics of Shark Management', *Acuity*, 1 December 2016.

7.   Sarah Gill, 'AFP exposes Australians to the risk of execution in foreign countries more often than you think', *The Sydney Morning Herald*, 3 September 2015 (www.smh.com.au/opinion/the-afp-peddles-injustice-by-helping-asian-death-penalty-states-20150902-gjdvu3.html).

8.   'The Campaign: George's General', *Time*, 11 October 1968 (http:// content.time.com/time/subscriber/article/0,33009,902367-1,00.html).

CHAPTER 2: TACKLING CLIMATE CHANGE

1.   Australian Bureau of Statistics (ABS), 'Labour Force, Australia, Detailed, Quarterly, Nov 2015', catalogue number 6291.0.55.003, 17 December 2015 (www.abs.gov.au/AUSSTATS/abs@.nsf/ DetailsPage/6291.0.55.003Nov%202015?OpenDocument).

2.   Laura Tingle, 'Malcolm Turnbull rejects coal ban as chief scientist talks zero emissions', *Australian Financial Review*, 27 October 2015 (www. afr.com/business/energy/malcolm-turnbull-rejects-coal-ban-as-chief-scientist-talks-zero-emissions-20151026-gkj8hi).

3.   See, for example, Sarah-Jane Tasker, 'Ivan Glasenberg takes swipe at Rio Tinto, says Glencore won't flood coal market', *The Australian*, 4 March 2015 (www.theaustralian.com.au/business/mining-energy/ ivan-glasenberg-takes-swipe-at-rio-tinto-says-glencore-wont-flood-coal-market/story-e6frg9df-1227247304912).

4.   International Energy Agency, *CO2 Emissions from Fuel Combustion 2012*, Organisation for Economic Co-operation and Development, Paris, 2012.

5.   Matt Canavan, 'It's right to consider Adani loan', *Australian Financial Review*, 7 December 2016 (www.afr.com/opinion/ its-right-to-consider-adanis-request-for-loan-to-help-build-railway- 20161207-gt5t9a).

6.   Mick Peel, Roderick Campbell and Richard Denniss, *Mining the Age of Entitlement*, The Australia Institute, Canberra, 2014 (www.tai.org.au/ content/mining-age-entitlement).

7.   Queensland Government, *Queensland Treasury Response to Commonwealth Grants Commission: Response to Terms of Reference for Commonwealth Grants Commission 2015 Methodology Review*, Queensland Treasury, Brisbane, 2013 (www.cgc.gov.au/index. php?option=com_attachments&task=download&id=1728).

8.   'National COVID-19 Commission (Advisory Board) Commissioners and Key Staff', National COVID-19 Commission Advisory Board, n.d. (https://pmc.gov.au/ncc/who-we-are).

9.   'PM Scott Morrison unveils plan for gas-led economic recovery', *ABC News*, 15 September 2020 (www.abc.net.au/news/2020-09-15/ morrison-unveils-plan-for-gas-led-recovery/12665020?nw=0).

10. Richard Denniss, 'Instead of taxing electric vehicles, heavy vehicles should pay more for the damage they cause', *The Guardian*, 25 November 2020 (www.theguardian.com/commentisfree/2020/ nov/25/instead-of-taxing-electric-vehicles-heavy-vehicles-should- pay-more-for-the-damage-they-cause).

11. Michael Mazengarb, 'Palaszczuk's secret royalties deal amounts to $270m loan to Adani, TAI says', *Renew Economy*, 2 October 2020 (https://reneweconomy.com.au/palaszczuks-secret-royalties-deal-amounts- to-270m-loan-to-adani-tai-says-56538).

12. Ian Verrender, 'How to engineer a gas-led coronavirus economic recovery and save $6 billion', *ABC News*, 24 August 2020 (www.abc. net.au/news/2020-08-24/gas-led-coronavirus-economic-recovery- national-covid19-comission/12587770).

13. Jim Stanford, 'Employment Aspects of the Transition from Fossil Fuels in Australia', The Centre for Future Work at the Australia Institute, December 2020.

14. See, for example, Cecilia Jamasmie, 'Glencore axes jobs, coal output at Australia's mine as price collapses', 7 December 2015 (www.mining. com/glencore-axes-jobs-coal-output-at-australias-mine-as- price-collapses).

15. Mark Hawthorne, 'Taunts in parliament and text brought about General Motors Holden's exit from Australia', *The Sydney Morning Herald*, 12 December 2013 (www.smh.com.au/politics/federal/taunts-in-parliament-and-text-brought-about-general-motors-holdens-exit-from-australia-20131211-2z6i6.html).

16. 'FactCheck: Do the Liberals have "a secret plan" to axe 20,000 public service jobs?', *The Conversation*, 24 July 2013 (https://theconversation.com/factcheck-do-the-liberals-have-a-secret-plan-to-axe-20-000-public-service-jobs-16032).

17. Cole Latimer, 'Mining Still Driving QLD Economy', *Australian Mining*, 13 December 2011 (www.australianmining.com.au/news/mining-still-driving-qld-economy).

18. ABS, 'Labour Force, Australia, Detailed, Quarterly, November 2020', catalogue number 6291.0.55.001, released 28 January 2021, Table 06 (www.abs.gov.au/statistics/labour/employment-and-unemployment/labour-force-australia-detailed/dec-2020#industry-occupation-and-sector).

19. Graham Readfearn, 'Queensland election: why the resources council's jobs figures don't pass "the laugh test"', *The Guardian*, 24 October 2020 (www.theguardian.com/australia-news/2020/oct/25/queensland-election-why-the-resources-councils-jobs-figures-dont-pass-the-laugh-test).

20. 'Is the mining industry the largest Indigenous employer? Check the facts', *Facts Fight Back*, 16 July 2013 (www.factsfightback.org.au/is-the-mining-industry-the-largest-indigenous-employer-check-the-facts).

21. ABS, 'Labour Force, Australia, Detailed, Quarterly, November 2020', Table 06.

22. Audrey Quicke and Ebony Bennett, 'Climate of the Nation 2020: Tracking Australia's Attitudes towards Climate Change and Energy', The Australia Institute, October 2020, p. 21.

23. Michael Bloch, 'Barnaby said stuff again', *SolarQuotes Blog*, 27 November 2020 (www.solarquotes.com.au/blog/barnaby-renewables-fossil-fuels-mb1778).

24. See state and federal government budget papers, and Deloitte Access Economics, *Estimates of Royalties and Company Tax Accrued in 2018–19,* report prepared for the Minerals Council of Australia, May 2020 (https://minerals.org.au/sites/default/files/Deloitte_Access_Economics-Royalties_and_Co%20_Tax_Estimates_Report_2018-19%20-%201%20Feb%202020.pdf).

25. Queensland Government, 'Budget Strategy and Outlook: Budget Paper No. 2', Queensland Budget 2020–21, Queensland Treasury, 2020, pp. 82, 89 (https://budget.qld.gov.au/files/Budget_Strategy_and_Outlook_2.pdf).

26. According to the Minerals Council of Australia, the entire minerals industry paid $39.3 billion in company tax and royalty payments in 2018–19. This figure includes the iron ore industry, which is much larger and more profitable than the coal industry. See Deloitte Access Economics, *Estimates of Royalties and Company Tax Accrued 2018–19*, report prepared for the Minerals Council of Australia, May 2020 (https://minerals.org.au/sites/default/files/Deloitte_Access_Economics-Royalties_and_Co%20_Tax_Estimates_Report_2018-19%20-%201%1%20Feb%202020.pdf).

In 2019, the healthcare and social assistance industry employed 1.7 million people, with average weekly earnings of $1243.40, for a total payroll of $109.9 billion. The education industry employed 1.1 million people that year, with average weekly earnings of $1262.70, for a combined payroll of $72.2 billion. Conservatively estimating an average income tax rate of 20 per cent means that employees of those two industries would generate around $36.42 billion in income tax. Conservatively assuming they paid GST on only half of their disposable income, they would pay a further $7.2 billion in GST, for a combined tax contribution of $43.5 billion. See ABS, 'Average Weekly Earnings, Australia', catalogue no. 6302.0, released 25 February 2021, Table 17 (https://abs.gov.au/statistics/labour/earnings-and-work-hours/average-weekly-earnings-australia/latest-release#data-download).

In short, the tax paid by the workers in the education and health industries is greater than the tax paid by the entire mining industry and, in turn, would likely be more than double the amount of tax paid by coal companies in Australia.

27. Tim Blair, 'Leader Followed', *The Telegraph*, 14 May 2012 (http://blogs.news.com.au/dailytelegraph/timblair/index.php/dailytelegraph/comments/leader_followed).

28. Marc Hudson, 'Tony Abbott, once the "climate weathervane", has long since rusted stuck', *The Conversation*, 9 October 2017 (https://theconversation.com/tony-abbott-once-the-climate-weathervane-has-long-since-rusted-stuck-84969).

29. ABS, 'Balance of Payments and International Investment Position, Australia, Sep 2015', catalogue number 5302.0, 1 December 2015.

30. Queensland Government Office of Economic and Statistical Research, 2015, 'International Visitors (a)(b) by Queensland Tourism Region, 2005–06 to 2014–15' (www.oesr.qld.gov.au/regions/far-north/tables/internat-visitors-qld-tourism-region/index.php).

31. Fidelis Rego and Rhianwen Whitney, 'Silver lining to mining boom's farm impact', *ABC News*, 15 November 2012 (www.abc.net.au/news/2012-11-15/silver-lining-to-mining-booms-farm-impact/4373268).

32. Larry Schlesinger, 'Sydney hotels surge to best performance in 20 years', *Australian Financial Review*, 15 December 2015 (www.afr.com/real-estate/sydney-hotels-surge-to-best-performance-in-20-years-20151214-glnk7c).

33. See 'FAQs', Independent Pricing & Regulatory Tribunal, accessed 19 February 2021 (www.ipart.nsw.gov.au/Home/About_Us/FAQs?dlv_FAQ%20List=(dd_Industries=electricity)).

34. '"Baseload" and renewable energy generation: exposing the myths', *Energy Matters*, 13 June 2018 (www.energymatters.com.au/renewable-news/baseload-energy-generation-expose-myth).

35. The Australia Institute, 'Breaking it Down: Victorian Coal Power Plants Least Reliable in Aus', media release, 12 February 2020 (https://australiainstitute.org.au/post/breaking-it-down-victorian-coal-power-plants-least-reliable-in-aus).

CHAPTER 3: WHAT REALLY CAUSES UNEMPLOYMENT?

1. '"If you have a go, you get a go": PM vows to make 2019 a winner for all', *SBS News*, 1 January 2019 (www.sbs.com.au/news/if-you-have-a-go-you-get-a-go-pm-vows-to-make-2019-a-winner-for-all).

2. Joe Hockey, 'Budget Speech 2014–15', Canberra, 13 May 2014 (https://archive.budget.gov.au/2014-15/speech/Budget_speech.pdf).

3. Melissa Clarke and James Bennett, '"Get a good job": Joe Hockey accused of insensitivity over advice to first-home buyers', *ABC News*, 9 June 2015 (www.abc.net.au/news/2015-06-09/joe-hockey-accused-of-insensitivity-over-sydney-house-prices/6532630?nw=0).

4. '"More than a million locked out of Jobkeeper"', *The Queensland Times*, 21 May 2020.

5. Tom Cusbert, 'Estimating the NAIRU and the Unemployment Gap', Reserve Bank of Australia, June 2017 (www.rba.gov.au/publications/bulletin/2017/jun/2.html).

6. ABS, 'Labour Force, Australia', catalogue no. 6202.0, released 21 January 2021, Table 1 (www.abs.gov.au/statistics/labour/employment-and-unemployment/labour-force-australia/dec-2020#data-downloads).

7. Latika Bourke, 'Joe Hockey's advice to first homebuyers – get a good job that pays good money', *The Sydney Morning Herald*, 9 June 2015 (www.smh.com.au/federal-politics/political-news/joe-hockeys-advice-to-first-homebuyers--get-a-good-job-that-pays-good-money-20150609-ghjqyw.html).

8. ABS, 'Labour Account Australia, September 2020', catalogue no. 6150.0.55.003, released 9 December 2020, Table 1 (www.abs.gov.au/statistics/labour/employment-and-unemployment/labour-account-australia/sep-2020).

9. Michael Pascoe, 'Beware the government punishing the poor for earning more', *The New Daily*, 30 June 2020 (https://thenewdaily.com.au/finance/work/2020/06/30/jobseeker-morrison-michael-pascoe).

10. Samantha Donovan, 'Indigenous "lifestyle choices" won't close the gap: PM', *AM*, ABC Radio, 11 March 2015 (www.abc.net.au/am/content/2015/s4195123.htm).

11. Peter Martin and Eryk Bagshaw, 'RBA governor Philip Lowe says wage growth too low, rates to climb but not yet', *The Sydney Morning Herald*, 11 August 2017 (www.smh.com.au/business/the-economy/rba-governor-philip-lowe-wage-growth-too-low-rates-to-climb-but-not-for-some-time-20170810-gxtb2l.html).

12. Karl Marx, *Kapital*, vol. 1.

CHAPTER 4: DEBT, DEFICITS AND BUDGET HONESTY

1. Commonwealth of Australia, 'Appendix D: Historical Australian Government Data' (https://budget.gov.au/2020-21/content/myefo/download/10_appendix_d.pdf).

2. Simon Birmingham, 'Australian Government General Government Sector Monthly Financial Statements December 2020', media release, 29 January 2021(https://www.finance.gov.au/publications/commonwealth-monthly-financial-statements/2021/mfs-december).

3. Ibid.

4. 'Social housing investment a win-win', Business Council of Australia, media release, 15 November 2020 (https://www.bca.com.au/social_housing_investment_a_win_win).

5.   Joe Hockey, 'The Case for Change – Address by the Hon. Joe Hockey
     MP, Treasurer', 23 April 2014 (www.liberal.org.au/latest-
     news/2014/04/23/case-change-address-hon-joe-hockey-mp-treasurer).

6.   National Commission of Audit, 'National Commission of Audit
     Releases Review of the Activities of the Commonwealth Government',
     media release, 1 May 2014 (https://parlinfo.aph.gov.au/parlInfo/
     download/media/pressrel/3142021/upload_binary/3142021.
     pdf;fileType=application%2Fpdf#search=%22media/
     pressrel/3142021%22).

7.   'Joe Hockey, Andrew Robb Transcript – Joint doorstop', 2 August 2013
     (www.liberal.org.au/latest-news/2013/08/02/
     joe-hockey-andrew-robb-transcript-joint-doorstop).

8.   'We've fundamentally honoured core commitments" says Tony
     Abbott', *7.30*, ABC TV, 4 December 2014 (www.abc.net.au/7.30/
     content/2014/s4142593.htm).

9.   Joe Hockey on *Q&A*, ABC TV, 19 May 2014 (www.abc.net.au/tv/qanda/
     txt/s3989246.htm).

10. 'Peter Costello slams Abbott tax plan as a "morbid joke"', *News.com.au*,
     14 April 2015 (www.news.com.au/finance/economy/peter-costello-slams-
     abbott-tax-plan-as-a-morbid-joke/story-fn84fgcm-1227302770409).

11. Paolo Mauro, Rafael Romeu, Ariel Binder and Asad Zaman, 'A Modern
     History of Fiscal Prudence and Profligacy', IMF Working Paper, Fiscal
     Affairs Department, 2013 (www.imf.org/external/pubs/ft/wp/2013/
     wp1305.pdf).

12. Catherine McGrath, 'Liberal leak damage', *PM*, ABC Radio,
     2 May 2001 (www.abc.net.au/pm/stories/s288187.htm).

13. See Transfield Annual Reports (various years).

14. Unconventional Economist, 'Is the Australian economy recession
     proof?', *Macro Business*, 10 September 2013 (www.macrobusiness.com.
     au/2013/09/is-the-australian-economy-recession-proof).

15. In announcing the peak in interest rates of 7.25 per cent in March
     2008, the governor of the Reserve Bank, Glenn Stevens, drew attention
     to the rapid growth in demand, which was outstripping the growth in
     productive capacity: 'Statement by Glenn Stevens, Governor: Monetary
     policy', media release, 4 March 2008 (www.rba.gov.au/media-
     releases/2008/mr-08-03.html).

16. Rod Myer, 'HILDA report shows home ownership sliding, incomes
     falling and inequality rising', *The New Daily*, 19 November 2020

(https://thenewdaily.com.au/finance/finance-news/2020/11/19/
hilda-report-inequality-rises).

17. Australian Government, 'Budget Strategy and Outlook: Budget Paper
No. 1', Budget 2015–16, Commonwealth of Australia, Canberra, 2015;
'Historical Data', Reserve Bank of Australia, accessed 19 February 2021
(www.rba.gov.au/statistics/historical-data.html); 'General Government
Debt', OECD, accessed 19 February 2021 (https://data.oecd.org/gga/
general-government-debt.htm).

18. Richard Denniss, 'Joe Hockey's penny-pinching will constrain growth',
The Age, 27 February 2015 (www.theage.com.au/comment/joe-hockeys-
pennypinching-will-constrain-growth-20150227-13qhy9.html).

CHAPTER 5: THE TRUTH ABOUT THE FREE MARKET

1. Andrew Tillett, 'Pacific central bankers warned not to backslide on
regulation', *Australian Financial Review*, 27 November 2020 (https://
www.afr.com/politics/federal/pacific-central-bankers-warned-not-to-
backslide-on-regulation-20201124-p56hez).

2. James Eyers, 'Afterpay's fees make it an "extortion scheme": Klarna
CEO', *Australian Financial Review*, 25 November 2020 (https://www.
afr.com/companies/financial-services/afterpay-s-fees-make-it-an-extortion-
scheme-klarna-ceo-20201124-p56hei).

3. ABS, 'Household Energy Consumption Survey, Australia: Summary of
Results, 2012', catalogue number 4670.0, 24 September 2013 (www.abs.
gov.au/AUSSTATS/abs@.nsf/DetailsPage/4670.02012?OpenDocument);
Jim Minifie, 'Super Sting: How to Stop Australians Paying Too Much
for Superannuation', Grattan Institute Report No. 2014-6, Grattan
Institute, Carlton, 2014.

4. 'Income for Medicare Levy Surcharge, Thresholds and Rates', Australian
Taxation Office, last modified 27 Oct 2020 (www.ato.gov.au/Individuals/
Medicare-levy/Medicare-levy-surcharge/Income-for-Medicare-levy-
surcharge,-thresholds-and-rates), Grattan Institute, Carlton, 2014.

5. Jared Owens, 'David Leyonhjelm declares war on nanny state', *The
Australian*, 26 June 2015 (www.theaustralian.com.au/national-affairs/
david-leyonhjelm-declares-war-on-nanny-state/story-fn59niix-
1227415288323?sv=269b8156e7f4031a81b36975114c4e93).

6. 'Fact Check: Does infrasound from wind farms make people sick?',
ABC News, 17 July 2015 (www.abc.net.au/news/2015-07-17/
wind-farms-david-leyonhjelm-fact-check/6553746).

7.   Paul Murrell, 'Changes to car import laws – Part 4', *Practical Motoring*, 5 July 2015 (https://practicalmotoring.com.au/car-news/changes-to-car-import-laws-part-4).

8.   Lisa Cox, 'Tony Abbott attacks ANU's "stupid decision" to dump fossil fuel investments', *The Sydney Morning Herald*, 15 October 2014 (www.smh.com.au/federal-politics/political-news/tony-abbott-attacks-anus-stupid-decision-to-dump-fossil-fuel-investments-20141015-116a0y.html).

CHAPTER 6: THE MYTH OF FREE TRADE

1.   'Australia Signs Landmark Free Trade Agreement with China', media release, June 2015 (www.exportfinance.gov.au/resources-news/news-events/latest-news/2015/june/australia-signs-landmark-free-trade-agreement-with-china).

2.   Productivity Commission, *Trade & Assistance Review 2013–14*, Annual Report Series, Productivity Commission, Canberra, 2015 (www.pc.gov.au/research/ongoing/trade-assistance/2013-14/trade-assistance-review-2013-14.pdf).

3.   ABS, 'Australian System of National Accounts, 2014-15', catalogue number 5204.0, 30 October 2015 (www.abs.gov.au/AUSSTATS/abs@.nsf/MF/5204.0).

4.   'China deal trades away jobs, rights', Australian Manufacturing Workers' Union, accessed 19 February 2021 (www.amwu.org.au/china_deal_trades_away_jobs_rights).

5.   Australian Fair Trade & Investment Network Ltd, 'Special rights for foreign investors to sue governments', AFTINET, accessed 19 February 2021 (http://aftinet.org.au/cms/isds-sue-governments-tpp-2013).

6.   Michael Brissenden, 'FTA: "Nothing's agreed until everything's agreed", says trade minister Andrew Robb', *AM*, ABC Radio, 27 July 2015 (www.abc.net.au/am/content/2015/s4281110.htm).

7.   'Andrew Robb on the Trans-Pacific Partnership', interview by Fran Kelly, *RN Breakfast*, ABC Radio, 29 July 2015 (www.abc.net.au/radionational/programs/breakfast/andrew-robb-on-the-trans-pacific-partnership/6655730).

CHAPTER 7: THE USE AND ABUSE OF ECONOMIC MODELLING

1.   Scott Morrison, 'Interview with Lisa Millar, ABC Breakfast', media release, 7 October 2020 (https://www.pm.gov.au/media/interview-lisa-millar-abc-breakfast).

2. Joseph Stiglitz, 'Information and the Change in the Paradigm in Economics', Nobel Prize Lecture, 8 December 2001 (www.nobelprize. org/nobel_prizes/economic-sciences/laureates/2001/stiglitz-lecture.pdf).

3. Jessica Irvine, 'Increase GST to 15 per cent and broaden to raise $256 billion: accountants', *The Sydney Morning Herald*, 20 July 2015 (www.smh.com.au/nsw/increase-gst-to-15-per-cent-and-broaden-to-raise-256-billion-accountants-20150714-gibmk6.html).

4. Ibid.

5. *Hunter Environment Lobby Inc v Minister for Planning and Infrastructure [No. 2]* (2014) NSWLEC 129.

6. Peter Abelson, 'Establishing a Monetary Value for Lives Saved: Issues and Controversies', WP 2008-02, Office of Best Practice Regulation Department of Finance and Deregulation, Applied Economics and Department of Economics, Sydney University, 2008.

7. Katharine Q. Seelye & John Tierney, 'E.P.A. drops age-based cost studies', *The New York Times*, 8 May 2003; Joseph E. Aldy & W. Kip Viscusi, 2007, 'Age Differences in the Value of Statistical Life: Revealed Preference Evidence', *Review of Environmental Economics and Policy*, vol. 1, no. 2, 2016, pp. 241–260.

8. Richard Denniss, 'Woolly Figures: An Analysis of the Treasury's Modelling of Emissions from Sheep and Cattle', Policy Brief No. 4, The Australia Institute, 21 October 2009 (www.tai.org.au/node/1574).

CHAPTER 8: WHAT CAN BE DONE?

1. Marie-Helene Martin, 'Equality begins in the creche', *The Guardian*, 19 February 2010 (www.theguardian.com/commentisfree/2010/feb/19/france-motherhood-childcare-equality).

2. See Tourism Research Australia, *State Tourism Satellite Accounts 2013-14*, Austrade, Canberra, 2015 (www.tra.gov.au/documents/Economic-Industry/State_Tourism_Satellite_Accounts_2013_14_FINAL.pdf); ABS, 'Census of Population and Housing' 2011 Census Data, access 19 February 2021 (www.abs.gov.au/websitedbs/censushome.nsf/home/historicaldata2011?opendocument&navpos=280&navpos=75&navpos=79).